At the Finishing Line

At the Finishing Line

A Primer for New Bindery Workers

by Frances M. Wieloch

GATFPress
Pittsburgh

GATF*Press*
Graphic Arts Technical Foundation
200 Deer Run Road
Sewickley, PA 15143-2600

Phone: 412/741-6860
Fax: 412/741-2311
Email: AWoodall@gatf.org
Internet: www.gain.net

Orders:

Online: www.gain.net

Mail: GATF Orders
P.O. Box 1020
Sewickley, PA 15143-1020

Phone (U.S. Only): 800/662-3916
Phone (Canada Only): 613/236-7208
Phone (all other countries): 412/741-5733

Fax: 412/471-0609

Dedication

This book is dedicated to my parents, Barbara and Matija Mavretic. They came to the U.S. with little formal education, but they never lost an opportunity to remind me "If you can read, you can learn anything."

Table of Contents

Preface

Although there may be some rare exceptions, printed material right off of a printing press inevitably needs to have something else done to it. Although "binding and finishing" form the most immediate description for these next steps, the "something else" that still needs to be done is really called "finishing." A run of flat printed material with extra margins and marks really does need to get to the finishing line.

Finishing may be as simple as trimming the edges of the printed sheets, cutting them apart, or folding them in half. Or finishing can mean cutting out intricate shapes, folding them, gluing them permanently to some pieces and less permanently to others, and then binding everything together in different versions meant for different locations.

The place where all this finishing takes place—the bindery—is becoming more technologically sophisticated. Automated in-line web press operations even blur the line between presswork and finishing. But there is no virtual reality in the bindery. The process, of necessity, remains one composed of very physical, mechanical operations on tangible objects in a very real three-dimensional—and cost-ruled—reality.

While many prospective workers disdain the mechanical aspects of bindery work, skilled bindery operators remain highly valued. But the skills that bindery workers need are changing. Mathematical and spatial ability and creativity remain constant, but it is no longer necessary for all bindery workers to be able to lift and move seventy-five pounds. The need for computer skills, however, continues to rise as new equipment replaces older models.

This primer touches on the basics of current bindery work to introduce it as a vital, interdependent part of the print production process to whoever needs to know about it—but especially to new and future bindery workers.

My personal hope is to carry on the theme of my dedication, so that anyone who reads this primer can learn about the basics of binding and finishing—and achieve success at the finishing line.

—Frances Mavretic Wieloch

Acknowledgments

It Takes a Team to Reach "The Finishing Line"

First-time book authors are usually allowed more acknowledgments than others. In that spirit, I would like to recognize the many people who helped this primer reach its finishing line. Following the philosophy of this book, I thank them back to front:

• First "in-line" for thanks are the pressroom workers at GATF. They operate as a team, taking on whatever presswork and finishing needs to be done. They are almost always neglected in public credit lines, and I want to thank them in the print they produce so well: Doug Bober, digital printing specialist; Ben Clark, multicolor press operator; Ned Herrick, estimator/production coordinator; John Krupa, bindery/pressroom assistant; Brian S. May, pressroom/bindery supervisor; John Morelli, digital and multicolor pressroom assistant; Rick Wagner, estimator/production coordinator; and Greg Workman, multicolor press operator.

• GATF's Center for Imaging Excellence (CIE) lived up to its name in providing answers to my questions, finding illustrations, doing preflighting, and more. For this my thanks go out to Julie Shaffer, CIE director, and prepress technologists Joseph Marin and Dave Dezzutti.

• Designing and editing are very different, but they complement each other in print production. Special thanks to editors Tom Destree and Amy Woodall and to designer Tracey Ryan. Their talents added immeasurably and seamlessly to this book.

• Special thanks are also due to GATF*Press* Publisher Peter Oresick, who gave me this opportunity; to Bill Farmer and Bruce Tietz, an eminently knowledgeable pair of GATF consultants who kept my binding and finishing feet on the ground; and to Jim Workman and Christy Semple for their contributions to the review and development of this primer as a component of the *GATF Bindery Training Curriculum.*

Binding and finishing operations are done at the end of the print production process—but they are affected by everything that was done before the binding and finishing stage, starting as far back as when the design decisions are made. To better understand binding and finishing, it helps to go back to the beginning, where the future of the print production process starts, and follow the process through its interconnected stages.

This chapter summarizes the graphic arts, or print production, process in four stages: design, prepress, presswork, and postpress. This summary is based on offset lithography, the printing process used for more commercial printing than any other. Although they have different ways of putting ink on the substrate, other print processes also follow these four stages of production. The chapter also focuses on a production process that is based on using digital files, called a *digital workflow*. (Publications such as the *GATF Encyclopedia of Graphic Communications* or *PrintScape: A Crash Course in Graphic Communications* offer explanations and details about other print processes and what happens in a non-digital workflow.)

Print Production: An Interdependent Process

How a printed piece is envisioned, set up in its digital file, and then imposed and printed will affect how it can be trimmed and otherwise finished. Even the material a job is printed on and how the material is handled after printing can affect binding and finishing.

Take, for example, what happened when a designer decided to create a foil-stamped and debossed (a process in which the image is sunk into the stock surface rather than raised above it, or embossed) piece printed on an expensive paper made of smashed tree bark. Unfortunately, the designer did not realize that the most important requirement for foil stamping is a flat, even surface on which to stamp. The tree bark paper was neither flat nor even. It was almost impossible for the bindery to stamp it, and the debossing was barely visible. Despite quality materials and great printing, the finished product looked second-rate.

The most successful print jobs—and the most cost-effective ones for print customers and also printers and finishers—are those that are designed "backwards," with binding and finishing (and distribution) as the first consideration. The farther along a print job is in the production cycle, the more time and materials have been put into it—and the more expensive it is to make changes or correct mistakes at each progressive stage. It is far less expensive to make design changes in a digital file than to reprint and rebind or refinish an entire job.

The Stages of Print Production

As stated earlier, print production can be divided into four main stages: design, prepress, presswork, and postpress.

Design

The design stage of a print job involves taking a communication idea and coming up with a physical depiction of it that will be reproduced using a printing process. This stage includes deciding

---

Comparative Cost of Making a Correction*

Design
On the computer during initial design....................$0.25
After a laser proof $1

Prepress
After a high-end digital color proof $30
After film production $100
After plate production $200

Presswork
On press ....$300–$1,000 and up

Postpress
After bindery ....$5,000 and up

*Note: The actual costs vary greatly from business to business, and the figures here are meant for comparison only.

- What purpose a printed piece will serve,
- What audience it will address,
- How and when it will be distributed,
- What words and images it will include, and
- What it will look like as a whole.

A print project moves through a variety of inter-connected stages in the production process on its path to completion.

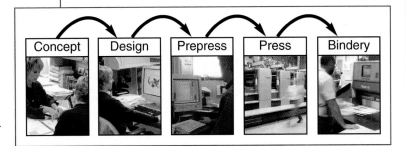

Concept | Design | Prepress | Press | Bindery

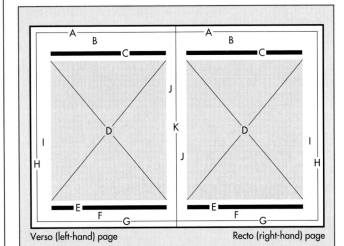

Verso (left-hand) page　　　　Recto (right-hand) page

Familiarize yourself with basic page terminology: (A) head trim; (B) top, or head, margin; (C) header; (D) body of the page; (E) footer; (F) bottom, or foot, margin; (G) foot trim; (H) face or front trim; (I) margin at the face, or front margin; (J) margin at the gutter; (K) fold.

Depending on the job's sophistication and its complexity—and also the customer's budget—the number of people involved in the design stage can be few or many. Design may involve only the ideas of the print customer and a graphic designer, or it may involve the input from the print customer, marketing experts, writers, editors, photographers, illustrators, several graphic designers, and even the printer, binder/finisher, and shipper.

The end result of the design phase is a digital design file that is meant to be printed. This file is created with page layout software like QuarkXPress, PageMaker, or InDesign. It contains all the pages and their elements (e.g., text in the chosen font, photography files, and line illustration files) in the correct sequence and placement.

Other software is used to create and manipulate the design elements within the page layout. Photoshop, for example, is used to manipulate photographic

Binding and Finishing Problems Can Start

In Design through:
- Neglecting to build in creep or thrust
- Neglecting to build in binding allowances for whatever binding process is to be used
- Improper grain direction—especially on cover or other heavy papers
- Failure to build in bleeds
- Failure to build in trim and fold lines

In Prepress/In Imposition by:
- Errors in pagination
- Using an incorrectly folded folding dummy
- Using a folding dummy made with the wrong stock
- Failure to account for lips
- Failure to account for grain direction
- Incorrect front-to-back alignment of images
- Combination layout that cannot be cut apart
- Inaccurate or missing trim marks
- Inaccurate or missing fold marks

During Presswork by:
- Failure to maintain sheet-to-sheet registration
- Failure to maintain front-to-back registration
- Quality control problems that decrease usable number of sheets
- Failure to print correct number of sheets of each signature
- In-line folder improperly set or doesn't hold register on web press
- Other in-line processes completed incorrectly

2

images, and Illustrator can be used to create line drawings.

In a digital print production workflow, the designed page layout file is what is sent to the printer, along with a proof—or several proofs, if necessary—showing what the file should look like when printed. Files and proofs can be sent to the printer by the graphic designer, the print customer, or both.

Prepress

The term *prepress* refers to the process of readying the job elements to be printed, and it can be described as what happens from the time a digital file has been completely designed until it is actually printed. Some printers and graphic arts service providers use the term "pre-media" to refer to the work done at this stage. This is especially true when their business is to prepare material to be published in other media in addition to print, including the Internet, CDs, DVDs, and audio and video formats.

The line between what is done and by whom can cross back and forth between the design and prepress stages. Because of the availability of equipment and software, graphic designers often do many of the jobs once done only by printers and prepress specialists, especially if the work is digital and meant to be published using several types of media.

At times, the printer receives a digital page layout file that includes all of the design elements and is meant to be considered "ready-to-print." At other times, prepress technicians at a printing facility or elsewhere will finish one or more steps (in addition to preflighting, described in the following paragraphs) needed to make the file print-ready. One example is that of scanning photographs, then creating and manipulating the high-resolution image files needed to reproduce the photos in print.

Prepress activities for print (in a digital workflow) can include preflighting, high-resolution scanning, imposition, film making, and platemaking.

Preflighting is a term borrowed from the aviation industry; it refers to the checks that pilots perform to make sure all of the plane's systems are working properly before takeoff. In the same way, prepress technicians check digital page

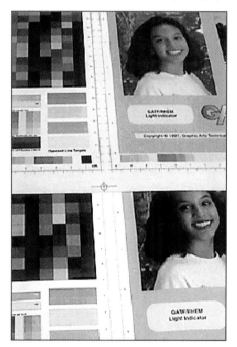

A color proof and press sheet.

Proofing

Proofing is done at every stage of the print production process, and it may even be done several times during one stage or another.

Proofs are used to test expectations as well as to predict them. Designers, for example, will "test" their ideas and the workability of their design files by making proofs. These proofs are usually output on laser printers, as many times as necessary, until the design is considered "perfect" by both the designer and the print customer. A design proof is sent to the printer along with the digital design file. The design proof is meant to show the printer what the designer/print customer expects the printed results to look like. The customer may also send a dummy of the proposed project to show expected folding or binding requirements. It may, in turn, be necessary for the bindery to prepare a dummy proof for the customer.

The printer also makes proofs. Prepress proofs make sure that the printer can use the design files to produce output that agrees with the customer's proofs, that color will reproduce as expected, that imposition is correct, that trapping is correct, and more. There is usually a final printer-made proof that both the customer and printer agree meets their print expectations. This is called a *contract proof,* and it becomes the customer-approved proof for the pressroom. With exacting jobs, customers may even attend the pressrun and "sign off on" (give their written approval of) printed press stock.

layout files for potential problems that could waste production time and materials. Preflighting can be done manually using a printed checklist or electronically using programs like Extensis Preflight Pro and Markzware

FlightCheck. Binding and finishing operations have also started to adopt the idea of preflighting jobs for potential problems.

High-resolution scanning involves using an electronic scanner to digitize photographic images and create computer files from them. The digital files can be manipulated using software like Photoshop and then saved for use in the page layout files or other files. In order for photographs to reproduce properly in print, the scanning resolution (image sharpness) needs to be high enough and also appropriate to the screen ruling, or lines per inch (lpi), at which the job will be printed.

Digital cameras are becoming more and more popular for capturing images for print because they eliminate the scanning step and can be easily used for both print and electronic publishing media. Digital camera images that will be printed must also be captured with a high enough resolution. These images are saved and manipulated in graphics programs like Photoshop for use in page layout files or other publishing media.

Imposition, which can also be called the *press sheet layout,* is the process of placing the print job graphics (page elements) where they need to appear on the printed press sheet. Job graphics can be entire pages, multiple copies of a label, or multiple copies of another element that isn't a literal "page." Press time and costs can generally be reduced when as many job graphics as possible are printed on the largest sheet possible.

Where the graphics need to appear on the press sheet hinges on a number of factors. Depending on the job, these factors can include the size of the press, the size and type of stock used for printing, whether any pages will form a signature (one or more printed sheets folded in

---

Workflow Management Support Materials

P F C   The GATF Preflight Checklist

All Preflight Technicians are to utilize this checklist to provide a thorough and consistent inspection of customer files.

The result of this examination will be a detailed Job Problem Report identifying the issues which will require correction.

Reviewing job as submitted for Preflight:
Carefully review the customer's materials: Do you have:
☐ Electronic files   ☐ Non-digital art (slides, illustrations, signatures, etc.)
☐ Customer's laser   ☐ Production Request Form completed by customer

Do you have the following information on the job jacket:
☐ Job number & customer name   ☐ Trim size of job (folded)
☐ Name of Salesperson/CSR   ☐ Bindery method (saddle stitch, perfect bound, etc.)
☐ Tentative proof due date   ☐ Inks to be used—don't forget varnish!

☐ Review the job jacket and compare it to the Production Request Form, check for discrepancies. Note any possible problems or sources of confusion on the Job Problem Report.
☐ Has the customer signed the copyright disclaimer on the Production Request Form?

Dealing with disks, folders, files and fonts:
☐ On your hard disk, create a folder entitled "Job Output".
☐ Within the "Job Output" folder, create a "job number—customer name" sub-folder.
☐ Write-protect any customer's floppies you may be working with.
☐ Determine supplied media format and compatibility—are you able to read this type of disk?
☐ Copy supplied customer's files to that sub-folder.
☐ Eject customer's disk and place in a safe place.
☐ Visually examine the customer's files. Are files compressed? Is there adequate disk space to decompress files?
☐ Within the "job number—customer name" sub-folder, create another sub-folder called "Originals"
☐ Check to see if customer included fonts for the job. If so, close all your fonts and activate the customer's fonts.

Launching the software, opening & preflighting a document:
☐ Launch the appropriate page layout program; open the document. Note missing fonts on the job problem report.
☐ Check the picture usage for broken links. Update "modified" images, but be very careful! Update images individually, and always click "Show Me", then watch the percentage, X Y coordinates and rotation numbers. If any of these change during the update, note the change on the Job Problem Report.
☐ If the files are present but the links are broken, close the document immediately without saving. Combine the page layout document and all the art/image files in a single folder. Next, open the document again. Now all links should be established (although some may need to be updated). When updating links, first choose "Show Me," then observe each image carefully to see if the position changes.
☐ Still missing some image files? Note them on the job problem report.
☐ Low-res files linked, but no hi-res exist? (Files with suffixes such as ".e," ".lay," or ".lo" indicate the use of OPI or APR. You'll have to locate the appropriate high-resolution files, or possibly make new high-res scans if the lo-res images are all the customer has.) Note the file names on the Job Problem Report.
☐ Change the target printer to the appropriate PPD and output resolution. Deselect unneeded PostScript effects.
☐ Before proceeding, choose "Save As" from the file menu! When the dialog box appears, add an extension to the name of the file to signify this file is to be used for output (such as ".rfo" or ".sbo"). Save this file in the first level of the customer job folder (outside the folder containing the art and image files).

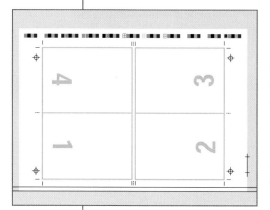

Page imposition on a press sheet that shows how, if the sheet is folded and trimmed, the pages would be in the proper sequence for the reader.

such a way that to form a multiple-page section of a book or pamphlet), what non-printed margins and allowances need to be left, and what binding and finishing processes will be performed.

Imposition in a digital print workflow is done using software like Scenic-Soft Preps, Dynagram DynaStrip, and Quite Imposing. During imposition, marks useful to binding and finishing the job are added. These marks include register marks (small guides placed on originals before reproduction to aid in positioning), trim lines, fold marks, spine/collating marks, cutting and scoring lines, perforation marks, and the like.

Of all the steps that take place in the prepress stage, imposition has the most direct effect on and interaction with binding and finishing work. If a piece is to be folded, imposition needs to be planned so that the piece is printed in the best paper grain direction (the alignment of fibers on a sheet) for any folds that will be made.

For example, folds made parallel to the grain direction are made more easily and have a sharper, cleaner crease. To experiment with this principle, try folding the flat face of a cereal box or a manila file folder; fold it first in a lengthwise direction, then separately in a crosswise one. It should be easy to decide which fold was made "with the grain." Next, make a fold with the grain and then a second fold against the grain on top of and at a right

angle to the first one. Then reverse the process and decide which folding sequence was better.

Scoring can, of course, help with folding, but it does not work with all materials, especially light-weight stock. Scoring is basically the process of creasing cardboard or a heavy paper along the fiber line for ease in folding or tearing. This will be discussed in more detail in Chapter Four.

Dummies, for folding and binding, remain essential tools for designers and binders, even in a digital print production workflow.

A *folding dummy* is made from a blank press-size sheet of the same stock used for the job. It is folded and marked with such information as page numbers to show how the pages should be arranged and Xs to indicate the gripper (lead) edge and side-guide edge when the work is printed on a sheetfed press. This dummy can also be used to determine which sides of each page need single-trim and double-trim allowances.

The *binding dummy* is similar to the folding dummy, but it is bound and trimmed to show what these operations will do to the printed stock. For saddle-stitched jobs, for example, it demonstrates

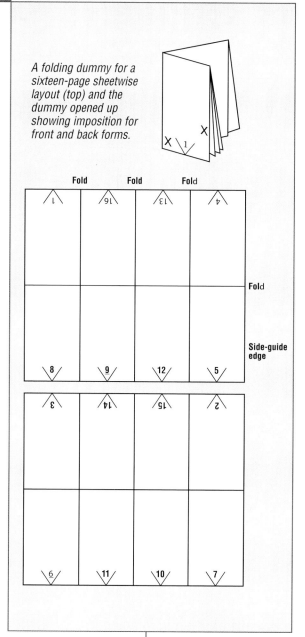

A folding dummy for a sixteen-page sheetwise layout (top) and the dummy opened up showing imposition for front and back forms.

5

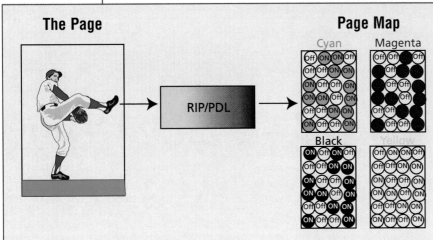

The Page → RIP/PDL → **Page Map**

Cyan | Magenta
Black | Yellow

The raster image processor (RIP) converts a file into a language the output device can understand—the cyan, magenta, yellow, and black dots that recreate an accurate representation of the image on press.

A film negative used in process photography.

how much of the margin is lost after stitching, and it shows how much compensation the designer and imposer need to allow for *creep* (outward movement of pages in the layout of book signatures as the press sheets are folded into one another).

Once the pages are imposed and the imposition has been proofed and approved, the imposed layout file may be handled in one of several ways:

- It may be output to printing-plate-sized film by an imagesetter and the film used to make the printing plates.
- It may be imaged directly onto printing plates by a platesetter.
- It may be imaged directly to plates already on a press.
- It may be printed without plates directly onto the stock by a digital press.

Imagesetting/film making is the stage in which imagesetters interpret, or RIP, the imposed digital files in a process called *raster image processing*. This process translates the image into the appropriate combination of dots, or spots, needed for conventional printing. Imagesetters use lasers to write these dots to paper that is output for proofing or to imposed sheets of film (also called film flats) that will be used to make the printing plates. Some imagesetters can also write directly to polyester printing plates.

Imagesetter film can be either negative or positive. Most U.S. printers use film negatives to produce negative-working plates. The European standard is positive-working plates.

The number of film flats needed to print a job depends on

- The number of press sheet sides to be printed, and
- The number of colors, spot colors, or special coatings to be applied to the press sheet.

If, for example, the job is made up of several pages, all to be printed with black ink on only one side of the press sheet, one imposed film flat and one plate are needed for printing (one film flat, one plate). Printing something different on the second side, also just with one ink, requires another film flat and another plate (two film flats, two plates). Multicolor printing using process colors needs four film flats and four plates, one for each primary process color (cyan, magenta, and yellow) and one for black, for each side of the press sheet.

Imagesetting is usually the responsibility of a printer's prepress department, but it can also be done by a prepress service bureau or a design house.

Platemaking is the step in a film-based workflow when imposed sheets of film from an imagesetter (or stripped film flats in an older, traditional workflow) are used to make the printing plates. To make plates, the film (which is made to the size of the printing plate) is placed in contact with a lithographic plate in a vacuum frame and exposed to light. The plate is then processed to make the image areas water-accepting and the nonimage areas water-rejecting for offset lithographic printing.

A *computer-to-plate (CTP) workflow* does not use film. The plates for the job are imaged in a dedicated platemaker. The platemaker uses lasers to write (to place or image) the printing spots directly to the plates from the information in the imposed digital files. Sometimes these plates need further processing before being hung on the press and sometimes they do not.

With *direct-imaging presses*, the plates, which are imaged directly from a computer file, are already part of the press. The Heidelberg Quickmaster DI, for example, has a roll of polyester plate material waiting to be imaged inside the press. In the future, presses may have reusable, re-imageable sleeves or plate materials that are part of the press.

Completely digital presses do not use plates at all but use an electrostatic (toner) system to print directly from a digital file to the substrate (the material to be printed on). These presses can do personalized printing and print a "quantity of one." Examples include the Xerox DocuColor, HP Indigo 3000, NexPress 2100, and Xeikon DCP 500.

Presswork

Presswork includes all the jobs needed to get the press ready to print, the printrun itself, and press washup afterward. Getting a press ready to print is called *make-ready,* and it includes such work as hanging the plates on the press, positioning the paper or other stock to feed into the press, filling the ink fountains, and making sure the press is printing the correct color and register for the job.

The pressrun, the operation that puts ink on the stock to create what we call printing, clearly depends on

the design and prepress work that come before it—but it, too, ties into binding and finishing. Presswork can also include some in-line finishing operations. This is often the case with webfed presses and includes cutting rolls of printed material into sheets and then folding the sheets into signatures.

The presswork stage and the way materials are handled

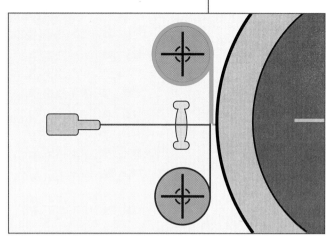

MAN Roland's DICOweb direct-imaging press uses a unique thermal transfer imaging "plate" technology in which ink-receptive material is transferred from a ribbon to a reusable steel sleeve.

can affect binding and finishing in several ways.

In one instance, a job was printed successfully but was over-dried at the end of the heatset web pressrun, and no re-moisturizing was done to the paper. In the rush to make the customer's deadline, the signatures (really "hot off the press") were immediately packed and shipped off to the bindery in sub-zero weather, further affecting the moisture content (of which there was probably none) and consequent brittleness of the paper. When the signatures started feeding through the saddle stitcher at the bindery, the folded edges cracked, and the pages literally flew all over the bindery.

Other press problems that would also affect binding and finishing might include:

Front-to-back misregistration and misalignment. This can be either an imposition problem, a press problem, or both. It is possible to misalign or misfeed sheets when

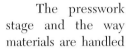

they are sent through a sheetfed press to be printed on the second side or to be perforated or scored on press.

Mishandling materials. If lifts of stock are mishandled and become "dog-eared," or if they are stored in the wrong temperature and humidity after printing, the stock may not feed properly into a folding machine.

Inadequately dried ink or varnish. This can also prevent printed stock from feeding properly into finishing machines. Or the press crew could unknowingly use an ink that is incompatible with a downline finishing/mailing process. For example, it can be impossible to successfully inkjet addresses on top of a high-ink-coverage job printed with a high-wax-content ink.

Postpress

The postpress stage of print production includes whatever happens after printing is finished. Just as with design and prepress steps, however, some finishing steps can overlap with presswork. This occurs with in-line setups in which some binding and finishing operations occur as a continuation of the pressrun rather than separately. The postpress stage includes binding and finishing operations and also shipping, mailing, or otherwise distributing the print job.

Printers who offer shipping and distribution services may offer them as completely separate services or include them with binding and finishing operations in the same area or close by.

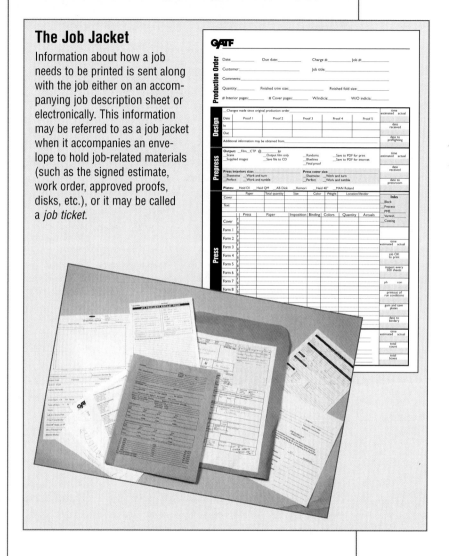

The Job Jacket

Information about how a job needs to be printed is sent along with the job either on an accompanying job description sheet or electronically. This information may be referred to as a job jacket when it accompanies an envelope to hold job-related materials (such as the signed estimate, work order, approved proofs, disks, etc.), or it may be called a *job ticket*.

It is common for even the most experienced people in print production to breathe a sigh of relief when a job has reached the bindery "at last." Getting to this point seems to be a signal that no more worry is needed because the job is almost complete. The bindery is the last stop before a job is shipped, mailed, or distributed—but binding and finishing are every bit as crucial to the final product as the earlier stages of print production. A lot of time, work, and money has already gone into the job, and a mistake here will be costly. While careless bindery work can ruin a well-designed and well-printed job, quick bindery thinking can sometimes salvage a job almost ruined because of design or printing mistakes—and top-notch binding and finishing can make a well-printed job a five-star winner.

What Is Binding and Finishing?

The sheets, rolls, and folded signatures that come off the press need to go through binding and finishing operations to make them into the products they are intended to be—folded pieces of paper, bound books and magazines, shaped boxes, and more.

The words "binding and finishing" are often used together, like an inseparable unit, to describe all the operations done to printing after the pressrun. Binding and finishing, however, are different yet overlapping activities.

Finishing is the more encompassing word. It covers post-printing operations like cutting, trimming, folding—and binding. It can also refer to special decorative operations like embossing, foil stamping, diecutting, and laminating and even to converting processes that change printed stock into another form, e.g., bags and boxes.

Binding describes the finishing work that is done to combine separate printed sheets or signatures and keep them together to make books, magazines, catalogs, and booklets. There are four basic categories of binding:

- Wire stitching, including saddle stitching and side wire stitching
- Adhesive binding, also called perfect binding
- Thread sewing and case binding
- Mechanical binding (as with binders and plastic combs)

It has been a continuing printing industry convention to call the place where any binding and finishing operations are done "the bindery." Some binderies prefer to call themselves "finishers," especially when they offer diverse binding and finishing services. This primer refers to "the bindery" to indicate where any binding and finishing work occurs, whether simple or complex and whether the work is done in the printing plant or a trade bindery or in a dedicated area or not.

Binding and finishing work may be done within the printing plant (in-house) or by external service providers, known as trade binderies. Binding and finishing work ranges from simple to complex and from manual and less automated to robotic and computer-controlled. One job may be as simple as folding a letter to fit inside a standard business-sized envelope. A complex children's pop-up book, however, may call for cutting, gluing, and folding intricate shapes onto pages, then binding them together in a laminated hard cover. Or the job may involve producing 100 or more different versions of the same magazine.

Binding and finishing can be done *in-line* in continuous operations, *offline* on separate pieces of equipment, or in a *combination* of continuous and offline operations. In-line finishing that continues directly from the pressrun is most

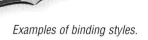

Examples of binding styles.

Bindery Workflow

Material arrives and is checked for quality
  and quantity
Preflighting checks for potential problems
Cutting and trimming
Folding (more trimming if needed)
  Knife folding
  Buckle folding
  Combination folding
Binding and trimming
  Saddle stitching
  Perfect binding
  Case binding
  Mechanical binding
Finishing (can occur at different times)
  Diecutting
  Embossing
  Hot foil stamping
  Inkjetting (can be done during binding)
Job is sent to shipping and distribution

The exact sequence of bindery work differs from job to job and bindery to bindery. This graphic simply shows where the basic operations fit. It does not take into account the many specialized types of finishing, especially those done in continuous or in-line operations.

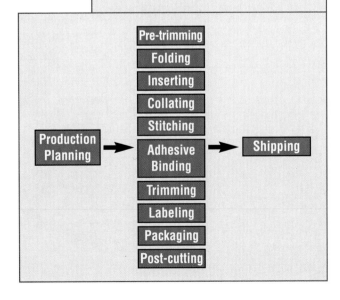

common with webfed and digital press operations. The trend in offline binding and finishing is to use multifunctional equipment and combine operations to make processes as continuous as possible.

Some printing businesses that do in-house binding and finishing specialize in a particular operation, say perfect binding, saddle stitching, or perhaps only casebound book binding. Others may offer basic finishing services in-house and send complex or extensive jobs to a trade bindery.

What Happens in the Bindery?

Bindery operations can seem complex because they can be combined and recombined to do a seemingly endless variety of tasks to produce an equally endless variety of print products. With a large bindery operation that handles many different types of jobs, it can be difficult to say exactly what needs to be done in exactly what order. A bindery that specializes in a single type of operation, however, may have a preset sequence of operations.

The flow of work through the bindery depends on the job, the availability of equipment, the efficiency of one binding or finishing sequence over another, the job completion date, and more. No matter how complex the job or the machinery, bindery operations fall under one (or several) of the following activities:

- Arrival of the printed material, which should be checked for quality and quantity and the presence of a job ticket or similar instructions. A job may go on to immediate processing, or it may need to be stored until all of the job components arrive or the right equipment is free.
- Preflighting, which can coincide with the job's arrival in the bindery.
- Cutting and trimming.

10

- Folding.
- Binding.
- Finishing, including specialty finishing and in-line finishing.
- Materials handling, which covers almost constant bindery operations that include moving, lifting, stacking, turning, jogging, and either storing jobs or packaging them and sending them to a shipping, mailing, and distribution center. Shipping, mailing, and distribution centers can be located within the printing plant or at an outside location.

Preflighting

As stated earlier, preflighting, or checking a job for possible problems before working on it, originally started in the prepress area, especially when digital workflows became popular. It is now becoming one of the first steps in bindery operations as well. A bindery mistake is always costly. On the other hand, if a prepress or press mistake has made it impossible to finish the job as specified, it is better to know before doing any finishing operations. And, knowing what the mistake is, the bindery workers may still be able to salvage the job by suggesting an alternative before it's too late.

A bindery preflighting checklist may help to confirm the following:

✓ All of the elements for the job have been delivered.

✓ The delivered quantity is correct.

✓ The material is in good condition. It has been checked for wet ink, excessive spray powder, sheet misregistration, setoff, web fold misregistration, drag marks from the press or an in-line folder, and sheet curl.

✓ The material has been temperature conditioned to match the atmosphere in the bindery.

✓ A job envelope, job ticket, or other instructions arrived with the job.

✓ Samples have been pulled for each signature or imposed component.

✓ Cut and fold marks are evident on the samples.

✓ Sample cuts have been made and will work as planned in the specs.

✓ A folding dummy has been made and matches the specs.

✓ A binding dummy has been made and matches the specs.

✓ The job has been inspected for prepress or printing mistakes that will affect the quality of the final product or the production rate. These mistakes can include:

　Page and press sheet layout errors
　Improper page positioning
　No compensation for creep
　Not enough bleed allowances
　Unevenly placed page numbers
　Not enough margin for the binding method
　Control marks inside the trim area
　Grindoff margin for binding miscalculated
　Ink or heavy printing in the glue area on the spine

Materials Handling and Automation

Bindery work is physical work. Loading, unloading, and maneuvering large lifts of stock and piles of signatures are constant activities, and they can be demanding. Automation and ergonomic enhancements, however, have made bindery jobs more efficient, less physically demanding—and open to a wider pool of potential workers. Where many job descriptions once specified the

11

Safety

Machines guards are now installed on all equipment, and electronic safety features are incorporated into most binding and finishing machines, but safe work habits and good housekeeping are essential as well. They protect both worker health and company profitability.

Besides knowing how to operate binding and finishing equipment—and operate it safely—bindery workers need to be aware of the following:

- Company safety policies and emergency procedures
- OSHA (Occupational Safety and Health Administration) standards for safe workplaces and practices
- Hazard Communication Standard, including requirements for chemical inventory, Materials Safety Data Sheets (MSDSs), container labeling, personal protective equipment (PPE), and employee training
  - Lockout/Tagout
  - Machine guarding
  - Forklift training and operation
  - Fire safety
- Ergonomics, or equipment and methods that reduce injuries like hearing loss, back strain, and repetitive motion disorders
- Personal safety practices such as tying back long hair or removing rings and dangling jewelry
- General housekeeping, plant conditions, and access to emergency communication and equipment

ability to lift seventy-five pounds, that figure is now often twenty-five pounds or less.

New bindery equipment is increasingly automated and increasingly multifunctional. It is also increasingly designed to fit into combined operations and continuous, one-pass processing rather than start-and-stop work.

Not all bindery equipment and binderies are automated to the same degree. One bindery may have completely automated, computer-controlled ergonomic equipment that is part of an integrated data system where machine functions are linked back to order entry. Another may blend manual technology with electronically controlled devices. Small binderies may find it efficient and economical to use manually operated machines.

Bindery automation encompasses a wide range of equipment and features, all as computer-controlled as possible. Automation ranges from pre-programmed menus on computer screens, stock lifts, air tables, and joggers to automatic feeders and "intelligent" collators that funnel ads or other inserts into regional versions of national magazines and catalogs. Paper cutters are pre-programmed with improved sheet handling information, bundler/stackers compress signatures into tightly strapped "logs," and robotic systems are available to load and unload pallets of printed material and transfer them directly from the press to the bindery or storage. And all binding and finishing equipment designed to handle jobs printed on digital presses is automated and computer-controlled.

What Are Cutting and Trimming?

Talk to a senior pressroom or bindery worker with many years of experience, and you may hear that person fondly refer to bindery work as "slicing and dicing." The more technical words, however, are "cutting and trimming." These words are sometimes used interchangeably, but they do refer to two different activities.

Cutting refers to operations performed to cut apart sheets of stock or printed material. In the bindery, cutting is almost always done using a single-knife guillotine cutter. Single-knife guillotine cutters differ from manufacturer to manufacturer, but they are large machines in which the knife is openly visible.

Cutting can be performed before printing or at different times in the binding or finishing process. Whether it is done specifically for binding and finishing reasons or for another reason, cutting is usually performed in the bindery because that is where the guillotine cutters are located. Stock may need to be cut to a different size before printing or trimmed to square it for sheetfed presswork. Sometimes rolls of paper are cut into sheets to be printed. This operation is called *sheeting* and is done on a machine designed for this purpose. Postpress cutting that is done to create a specific pattern, for example to shape a box that will be assembled later, is referred to as "die-cutting" rather than cutting.

In the binding and finishing process, cutting flat press sheets apart is often one of the first jobs done in the bindery. It may be done to separate multiple copies of the same image printed on the same sheet or to separate signature pages.

Trimming refers to operations done to
• Neaten the ragged edges of printed pieces,
• Open the closed edges of folded signatures, and
• Bring printed material to its designed size.

Trimming can be done using a dedicated three-knife or five-knife trimmer or a single-knife guillotine cutter. The knives and movable parts of dedicated trimmers are usually enclosed in a box-like housing. Trimming using a dedicated trimmer tends to be an in-line operation. Three-knife trimming machines trim three sides—front, head, and tail—in a combined operation.

Cutting and trimming machines almost always use guillotine-type cutters with knives that descend to cut the material. The machines can be manual or electronic.

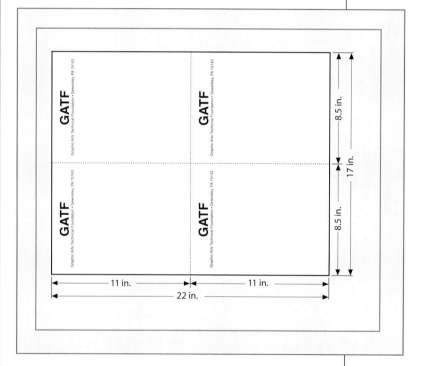

An 11×17-in. (432×559-mm) sheet size allows four 8.5×11-in. (216×279-mm) letterheads to be cut out of one sheet of paper with no trim waste.

Rotary blade cutters are also used, and they are found mostly in large, sophisticated in-line web press operations.

Cutting and trimming can be done offline and separately from printing and binding, or they can be done inline as part of a continuous process. Web presses, for example, usually have a unit at the end of the press that cuts the web roll apart into sheets of signatures and also folds the signatures.

Components of Guillotine Cutters

Guillotine cutters can be found in almost every printing operation, small to large. They are available in different models and sizes, but all have the following: a knife, cutting stick, table, side and back gauges, and a clamp.

The **knife,** which is long and heavy, is bolted to a bar mounted near the front of the machine. The bar and knife move up and down. To make a cut, the knife descends from its raised position to the table of the machine, slicing through a stack of paper or other stock.

The most commonly used knife is the standard steel knife, which is easy to grind and hone. Knives are also made of high-speed tool steel. These knives are more expensive than standard steel knives, but they are also more abrasion- and impact-resistant. Different knives can be purchased to handle materials of different hardnesses.

Carbide-insert knives have steel backings with pieces of carbide soldered or braised into them. They cost more to purchase and regrind, but manufacturers are working on coatings that will extend the cutting life of these knives. Carbide-insert knives are used to give a clean cut to labels and other special jobs.

The **cutting stick,** an important cutter component, fits into a narrow groove on the cutter table right below the knife. Every time the knife slices through a pile of stock,

it touches the cutting stick, usually made of a hard plastic material, instead of the metal table. This prevents the knife from breaking or becoming dull too quickly. The cutting stick needs to be turned over or replaced when the knife has dug into it so deeply that the last sheet in the pile is torn instead of cut. Some binderies follow a regular knife maintenance and replacement schedule instead of waiting until a job is badly cut.

The **side and back gauges** of the guillotine cutter position the stock under the knife, squaring it before cutting. The side gauges are stationary; the back gauge can move to accommodate different cutoff lengths.

A back gauge that is divided into two or more segments is called a *split gauge.* A guillotine cutter with a back gauge divided into three sections can be used to trim books at the top, bottom, and one side without changing the setting. Most bound jobs, however, are trimmed on dedicated three- or five-knife trimmers installed in-line

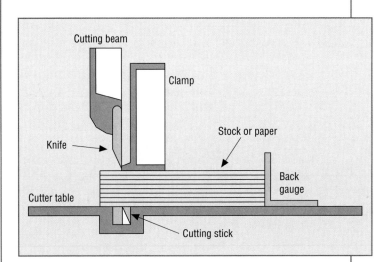

Principal parts of a guillotine paper cutter.

with binding equipment. These trimmers cut the top, bottom, and side of the bound sheets in one operation.

The **cutter clamp** is a metal bar that runs parallel to the knife. It has two functions: (1) to expel air from the pile of sheets before it is cut and (2) to hold the pile firmly in place during cutting.

Soft material requires a high clamping pressure; hard material, a low clamping pressure. Stocks of average hardness, such as writing paper and common printing paper, can be processed with a medium clamping pressure. Up-to-date cutters modify the clamp pressure electronically and automatically adjust to the correct clamping pressure.

Operating the Cutter

Safety first. Because guillotine machines are such powerful cutters, they have built-in safety features.

Two hand controls, well out of the way from the knife, must be operated simultaneously to start cutting. They are wired so that releasing either hand control instantaneously stops the knife with a brake. Electronic eyes also monitor the cutting area and stop cutter operation if anything interrupts the path of the light beams.

Some additional safety tips:

- Check the safety bolt and brake action at the start of the work shift and before resuming production after a break period.

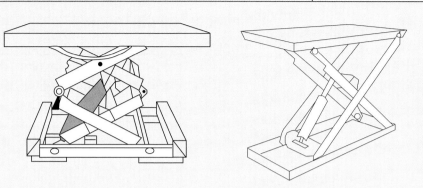

Left: A portable lift that maintains optimum height with hydraulics. Right: A load leveler that maintains optimum height with springs.

Tip Sheet: Cutting

Procedures vary from bindery to bindery, so the following steps are only general guidelines:

- Make sure you have the job ticket or cutting instructions and that the instructions match the stock to be cut.
- Check the register marks on the printed sheets carefully before beginning a job since register accuracy during the pressrun affects the success of cutting.
- If the art or type margins are tight, check for imperfections right away to prevent loss of imagery or improper alignment during trimming.
- Confirm the cutting instructions by making a sample cut.
- Place the pile on a stock table, press skid, or automatic lift and/or jogger and set the cutter controls for the first cut. How you set the controls will depend on the job, the machine, and your company's procedures.
- Quality cuts and top machine productivity depend on choosing the correct knife cutting angle. This angle depends on the characteristics of the material to be cut. No single angle is universally suited to all materials, but a narrow angle is considered best for soft materials and a wide angle best for hard materials.
- Jog the lift to align the guide edges and prevent the sheets from sticking together.
- Transfer the pile to the cutter. This operation can be less or more automated, and some cutters are loaded from the front and some from the back.
- Stack the lift against the side and back gauges, then activate the clamp and knife to begin cutting the sheets.
- Remove waste frequently. Many cutters have attachments that automatically remove waste stock and even bundle and store it for disposal.

15

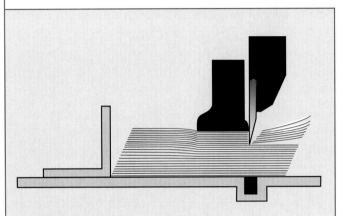

Illustration of an overcut.

Tip Sheet: Cutting Different Materials

Soft materials can be difficult to cut simply because they are soft. They have poor sliding properties and may wedge in front of the knife. Soft materials also have a high air volume in the pile, and so they can easily be **overcut.** This means that the sheets on the top are cut shorter than the lower layers. To prevent this, use a narrow cutting angle and a knife with a smooth finish.

Carbonless paper, a chemically coated stock for making duplicate copies of business forms (e.g., credit card receipts) without using carbon-covered sheets, is a difficult-to-cut soft material because it can be so easily marked. Too much clamp pressure marks the whole pile. Too little clamp pressure produces an inaccurate cut. Experimenting may be needed to determine the best clamp pressure. A sharp knife is also essential.

Hard materials like art paper, cardboard, or foils may deflect and damage the knife during the cut. In most cases, this is caused by using a cutting angle that is too narrow. Overcutting and under-cutting (short cuts when the clamping pressure is weak) are both problems with hard materials. Stock that varies in thickness can tend to bulge outward from the center because both ends are pulled out by the knife and clamping pressure is insufficient.

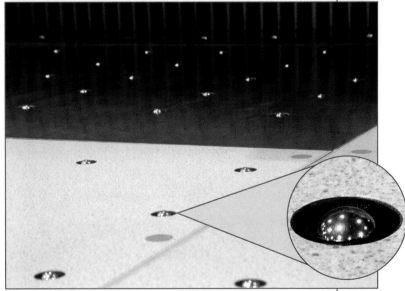

Top: A cut line indicator uses a light source to shine a thin line of light on the positioned paper pile, showing exactly where the cut will be made.

Bottom: Close-up of a cutting table and inset close-up of a roller.

- Never disconnect or alter the two hand controls in any way.
- Do not reach under the knife to remove scraps or to straighten a lift.
- Keep the floor around the machine free of paper, wipes, and tools.
- Avoid distractions.

It is important to have and check the cutting instructions before making the first cut. These instructions can be sent electronically and/or be shown on a job ticket or cutting card. Some companies have checklists and even preflighting procedures for binding and finishing operations.

Making the wrong cut can ruin the entire job, which may need to be reprinted at considerable cost to a company's bottom line.

Knife Maintenance

A dull knife cannot make clean, accurate cuts. One sign of a dull knife is that the cutter strains to slice through a pile. Inaccurate and ragged cuts also indicate that the knife needs to be resharpened. If the edges of the paper are rough, stick together, and have a darker color, the knife has become blunt. Under this condition, the knife slices through the last sheet of a hard material with a sharp bang against the cutting stick.

Frequent resharpening is economical for several reasons:

- Sharpening costs less when the knife wear is slight rather than extensive.
- Sharp knives significantly improve cutting quality.
- Fewer knives need to purchased if they are resharpened regularly and properly.

- Wear and tear on the guillotine cutter is reduced when the knife is sharp.

Automatic devices like the built-in knife lift have made it easier to change cutter knives and easier for a single operator to do so. On larger guillotine cutters, it may take two people to change the knife. All power is locked out during knife changing. On some machines, however, the power remains on so that an operator can use the clamp to help during knife changing. With these machines, however, the knife circuit itself is deactivated.

Tip Sheet: Knife Maintenance and Protection

- To protect the cutting edge, store the knife in its box until it is needed.
- Do not place a knife on the machine table without using cardboard or wooden supports.
- Keep the knife's surface and beam completely free of dirt and burrs.
- Make sure the threaded holes in the knife and the screws used to seat it are in perfect condition.
- Tighten all knife screws lightly at first to avoid damage during the final "firm" tightening.
- After inserting a new or resharpened knife, remove all hand tools from the cutter table.

17

The folding that happens in the bindery is not what card players do during a card game. On the other hand, knowing when to fold is something both card players and bindery workers do need to know, as it might need to be done before or after cutting, or with or without scoring.

What Is Folding?

Folding is the process of bending printed stock over on itself and making creases that will not readily rebound and undo themselves. Printed stock is folded for many practical and design reasons. Some of the more common reasons for folding materials are to:

- Prepare material to be mailed in a particular size envelope or to be sent as a self-mailer.
- Create products that unfold to reveal their printed contents, e.g., marketing pieces, brochures, newspapers, magazine inserts, greeting cards, and maps.
- Make signatures that will be collected in order, bound together, and trimmed to become booklets, magazines, catalogs, and books.

Samples of folded products.

Folding is used to create single-unit pieces or to create signatures that will be bound together. The folding done to make three-dimensional boxes and similar products is part of a special area of print production called *converting*, and it is not covered in this primer.

In print production, folding is done mechanically by machines that are increasingly computer-controlled. Hand folding is also done, but binderies try to avoid this

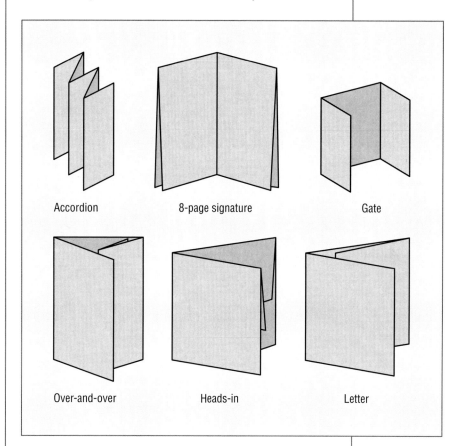

Accordion   8-page signature   Gate

Over-and-over   Heads-in   Letter

A selection of common folding styles.

19

labor-intensive, expensive process. Hand folding, however, may be used to finish a short run, to finish the last fold or folds on a complex job, or even to correct for a design or imposition-stage mistake.

Machine folding uses one of two basic folds, a right-angle fold or a parallel fold. A right-angle fold is made by folding the sheet in half, rotating the sheet halfway, then folding it in half again. Additional right-angle folds can be made as needed. Try this with different sizes and thicknesses of paper to see what happens and why some stock may need to be scored. One fold makes four pages (sides), two folds make eight pages, and three folds make sixteen pages, etc.

A basic parallel fold is made by folding a sheet of paper twice in different places but along the same direction.

Numerous configurations can be made from combining right-angle and parallel folds. A larger variety of folds than most people realize is used for printed products. *FOLD: The Professional's Guide to Folding,* for example, details step-by-step setup instructions (including those for the digital design file), uses, features, and hints for more than two hundred types of folds.

Signature Folding

A signature is a single press sheet that has several pages printed on both sides of it. It is meant to be folded to form a group of pages that will appear in their correct order in a book or a magazine. Signatures may consist of four pages (sides), eight pages, sixteen pages, or some other multiple of four. Planning for this arrangement takes place during the prepress stage of print production and is called *imposition.* The binding method (e.g., saddle

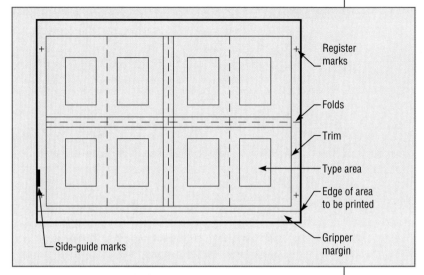

Sample imposition layout showing basic elements that indicate how images should be assembled on a press sheet to meet press, folding, and bindery requirements.

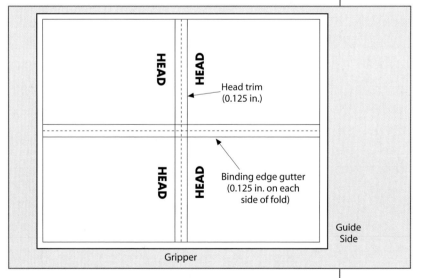

Sample imposition for perfect binding showing the gripper edge, side guide, and binding edge gutter.

Close-up of a product that has undergone scoring.

How to Score

Scoring is used to create smooth, strong folds, to reduce or eliminate cracking, or to determine a fold's precise location. It is typically used on stock that is difficult to fold or has a tendency to crack. It may also be used on jobs with critical cross-grain folds or with heavy or solid ink coverage where the fold needs to be made.

Scoring can be done several ways, but it essentially places a narrow ridge in the stock.

Litho scoring, the least expensive method, is done in-line on the printing press using a flexible scoring rule on the impression cylinder. The stock travels through the press between the blanket and the impression cylinder and is embossed by the rule. This type of scoring may not be precise enough for certain high-quality jobs.

Letterpress scoring is done on the same type of machines used to foil stamp and emboss. The presses use either a male die and matrix set or a scoring/creasing rule and channel-creasing matrix to raise a ridge on the inside of the fold. This is the method currently favored for creating high-quality folds and preventing cracking.

Rotary scoring uses a wheel and is usually done during offline folding. This type of scoring can be done with a single-shaft scorer or one that makes two scores.

Wet scoring is used mainly on uncoated stocks to make them more pliable. It is done on a paper-folding machine using a device that injects a mixture of isopropyl alcohol and water along the area to be folded. This method is not recommended for coated stocks because the wetting solution tends to bead up on the coating rather than penetrate the fibers.

Tip Sheet: Scoring

- Scoring can be done in any grain direction, but it is riskier to do so against the paper grain or across areas with heavy ink coverage. Generally, the smoothest folds run parallel to the grain. Cross-grain folds are more likely to produce buckling and cracking, but they are also stronger and more flexible.

- If the piece will contain inserts or multiple signatures, adjust the width of the score to account for the extra material. The heaviest weights of stock may need two parallel scores, also called a double score.

- Regardless of the scoring method, the score should be wider and deeper than the thickness of the paper, and it should be made so that the hinge will be on the inside of the fold.

- UV-coated products are considered the toughest to score and fold.

- Heavy uncoated papers, book stocks over 80 lb., and all cover stocks generally benefit from scoring.

- Any job with full ink coverage over the fold area must be scored to avoid damaging the ink film.

- Any job with more than four folds needs up-front planning among the print customer and designer, the printer, and the bindery.

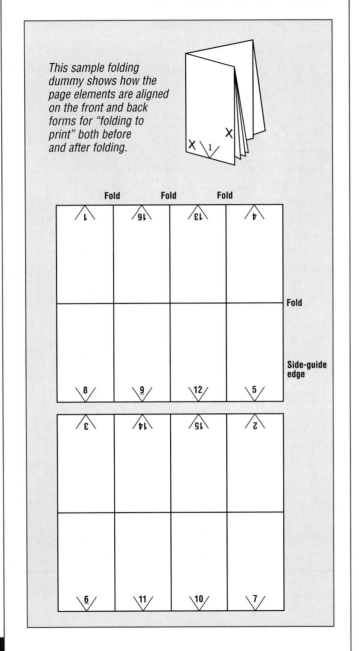

This sample folding dummy shows how the page elements are aligned on the front and back forms for "folding to print" both before and after folding.

stitching vs. perfect binding or case binding) will affect the imposition and assembly order.

Printed signatures have fold marks, indicated by broken lines, that are used to set up the folder. The goal is to align all the headers, footers, and image areas from page to page and from one signature to another. Backup registration from the front side to the reverse is important. When signatures are folded to form groups of pages printed on both sides, the process is called "folding to print." Folding press sheets with printing on only one side of the form is called "folding to paper." Folding to paper is often done on pieces that will stand alone. Backup register is not a consideration when folding to paper.

Signatures printed on web presses are usually folded in-line by a machine at the end of the web press. Signatures printed on sheetfed presses are folded offline by machines separate from the press.

Folding Machinery

Folding machines are either knife folders or buckle folders, and they can also be a combination of the two. Knife folders make only right-angle folds. Buckle folders make both parallel and right-angle folds. Combination folders incorporate both knife folding and buckle folding mechanisms.

Knife Folders

Binderies that specialize in folding large sheets, especially to produce book signatures for case binding, usually use knife folders. Knife folders are also well suited for gatefolding heavier-weight stocks. The machines are called *knife folders*, or sometimes *right-angle folders*, because they use metal blades to force the stock through a set of rollers to make folds that are always at right angles

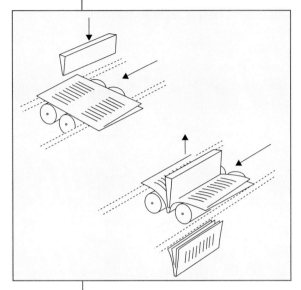

Knife folder.

to each other. Some knife folders also have sections that can do parallel folds.

Knife folders are constructed of individual folding units, or stations, at several levels. Each unit is located at a right angle to the preceding one, and each folding station makes only one fold.

Knife folders use tape-style conveyor belts to carry the stock from the feeder to the first folding station and then to subsequent stations for as many folds as necessary. Each folding station has a vertically moving knife and two rollers operating in different directions. The stock is stopped at each station by a gauge and positioned against a side guide. The knife comes down and pushes the stock between the two rollers, and the stock is pinched to form the fold. The rollers are adjusted to fit the thickness of the stock going through them. The folded piece then descends to the next level, where it is conveyed to the next folding station. The process is repeated until the desired number of folds is made.

Most knife folders are also equipped with perforators that pierce the folds to make holes. This lets air escape and helps prevent wrinkles. Other attachments include photoelectrically controlled devices that bind small brochures with an adhesive instead of wire staples, devices that provide scoring capability, slitters that cut apart jobs run in multiples of two or more, and edge

Perforated products, such as this postcard, should be able to tear easily.

Perforation

Perforating, or *perfing* as it is sometimes called, is the process of mechanically slotting or punching tiny holes into paper or board. Perfing is done to permit part of a sheet or page to be detached, to provide a guide for folding, to allow air to escape from signatures, or to prevent wrinkling when folding heavier papers.

Perforating is done one of three ways, with:

- A slotted wheel on a folder
- A perforating rule (an L-shaped slotted strip of steel) applied to the impression cylinder on an offset press
- A comb-like cutting rule on a letterpress machine

Perforations are referred to as *standard, mini,* and *micro* depending on the number of perfs per inch. A standard perf can measure 8 per inch while a micro perf measures 72 per inch.

23

Sample perforated product.

Tip Sheet: Perfect Perfs

• Try to avoid perforation too close to any final trim edges.

• Make sure there is room for error if a perforation registers with any printing.

• Consider perforating the spine and head of signatures that will be perfect bound to allow trapped air to escape, reduce paper wrinkling, and improve clamp grip during binding. Perfs should be numerous enough to easily let out trapped air, but not so deep that the sheets separate under finger pressure. Perfs that separate too easily can cause binding problems.

• When case binding, never perf the spine side of a signature.

Samples of scored, perforated, and slit sheets.

trimmers that open the closed folded heads of signatures in-line.

The most frequently encountered knife folder designs are the jobber, the double-sixteen, and the quadruple.

The *jobber* has four right-angle folding levels and one or two parallel sections. This jobber can be set up to make up to four right-angle folds, two right-angle folds with a third fold parallel to the second, or three right-angle folds with a fourth fold parallel to the third. This flexibility makes the jobber the most popular knife folder.

The *double-sixteen folder* can make two sixteen-page units separately or, when the units are inserted one within the other, it can produce a single thirty-two-page unit. Adding a double thirty-two-page section to this machine makes it possible to produce two (smaller) thirty-two-page signatures. The double-sixteen is used mostly for publication work.

The *quadruple folder* makes four sixteen-page units separately or, when the units are inserted within each other, it can produce two thirty-two-page units. The units made from a single sheet will have closed heads that need to be trimmed open. The quad is used mostly in edition (or case) binding sewn hardcover books.

Buckle Folders

Buckle folders feature continuous stock feeding and are characterized as high-output multipurpose machines. They can handle most folding assignments and are considered easy to set up and run. Their individual folding stations are modular, and new folding capabilities can be added to existing equipment. Each folding station can have up to six buckle plates, arranged alternately above and below each other. The folding stations can also be operated as independent stations, either hand-fed or fitted with a sheet feeder. Most printers with binding

The press sheet entering the first buckle plate on the buckle folder.

equipment have at least one buckle folder; trade binders use them extensively.

The folding mechanism on a buckle folder consists of three rollers and a buckle plate. Two rollers are horizontal and one is stacked vertically. The two vertically stacked rollers carry the incoming stock into the buckle plate until it reaches an adjustable stop. This feed stop keeps the lead edge of the stock from moving forward. The stock itself, however, keeps feeding forward. This movement "buckles" the stock at a specific point, producing a bulge that is caught between the two horizontal rollers to form the fold. The stock passes between the rollers and is conveyed to the next station.

Sheet deflectors can be inserted to bypass any buckle plates not needed for a particular folding job. Buckle-plate folders are known for being best suited for handling parallel folding and lighter-weight stock. Buckle folders can, however, be set to produce one or more right-angle folds. Newer buckle-plate throats and folder rollers are designed to handle a variety of stocks.

Combination Folders

Combination folders integrate the folding mechanisms of buckle folders and knife folders. In its most common configuration, the first section of a combination folder consists of several buckle fold plates, with the remaining sections having right-angle folding knives. The ideal application for combination machines is folding medium-size sheets, which often are designed with several different folds.

Combination folders make parallel folds with the buckle plates in the first folding station. The knife folder section makes any right-angle folds. Buckle plates are also used for folds parallel to the first right-angle fold. Conveyor tapes move the stock through the folder.

Combination machines fold heavier stock with less difficulty than buckle folders because the bulk of a folded piece does not have to pass through as many rollers and stock grain is less of a problem.

Because the units of combination folders are stacked instead of at right angles to one another, these machines need less floor space than all-buckle machines. The parallel section of a combination folder is similar to that of other folders, and it can produce the same folds as an all-buckle machine with a similar number of plates. Combination folders are, however, limited in their ability to handle right-angle folds.

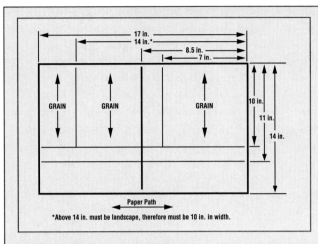

Showing grain direction with fold.

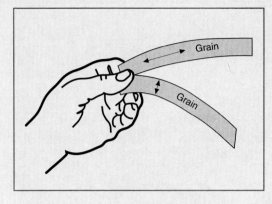

Flex test for determining grain direction.

Tip Sheet: Folder Operation and Folding

• Before starting any folding job, first check the folding instructions or job ticket information following your company procedures. You may have a sample folding dummy to follow, but it is also wise to make a folded sample from the printed stock.

• Post a makeready list for each folder on or near the folder.

• As with all other binding and finishing equipment, make sure you know how to operate the folder properly and safely.

• Sheet deflectors that are worn or positioned too low on a buckle folder can snag sheets as they pass by, causing a bent corner, called a dog-ear. To determine which deflector is causing the problem, examine the dog-eared sheet as it comes off the unit. If the corner is bent down, it is snagging on one of the bottom plates; if it is bent up, one of the upper plates is causing the problem. Adjust deflectors that are too low by moving the screws on the end of the deflector upward. If the deflector is worn, replace it.

• To avoid excessive static electricity, do not install folders in direct drafts (near doorways and air vents). Occasional problems caused by static electricity can be controlled by increasing the bindery's relative humidity to 50–55% when the room temperature is between 70–80°F. If the bindery is not air-conditioned or moisture-controlled, any of the following suggestions may help:

• Make sure the machine frame is grounded.

• Place "tinsel" (a material that breaks up static charges) across the register table and feeder.

• Spray antisetoff powder or silicone on the register table of the folder.

• Cover printed jobs with plastic whenever binding will be delayed.

• A buildup of antisetoff spray powder, small particles of paper, and other dirt and dust can keep rollers and gears from meshing properly. It is a good idea to schedule regular maintenance to clean and lubricate the folder according to the manufacturer's specifications.

• Paper folded with (parallel to) the grain offers less resistance. Accordion-fold brochures, books, and other bound materials should have the grain running parallel with the binding. The pages will be easier to turn and the piece will lay flatter.

• Paper folded against the grain is more durable under stress. When planning how a piece comes together, try to fold against the grain for "active" folds that will be opened and closed frequently, such as the spine of a brochure or pocket folder.

When it comes down to binding, binding can come down to the wire—wire stitching, that is. There are two forms of wire stitching: saddle stitching and the less common side-wire stitching.

Saddle and Side-Wire Stitching

With saddle stitching, wire is driven through the center fold (gutter) of a signature or group of signatures to form thin booklets, brochures, folders, and leaflets. The term *saddle stitching* comes from the way the staples are applied to the signatures as they lay draped open on a "saddle" bar on the binding machine. The cover and body are stitched at the same time, even if the cover is heavier. Stitching is usually followed by trimming the top, bottom, and front edges of the printed piece.

It is easy to find examples of this popular method of binding. It is used to bind magazines like *Time* and *Newsweek* and to bind catalogs, annual reports, and all sorts of booklets. Saddle-stitched publications open easily and lie flat.

The other type of wire binding, called *wire-based side stitching*, is becoming less common because the pages don't open flat and stay open. With this type of binding, the wire staples are driven into and along the binding edge, or the backbone, of a group of pages. Side-wire stitching has been mostly replaced by perfect binding with adhesives.

Planning a Saddle-Stitching Job

Saddle-stitched jobs need specific pre-planning at the design and prepress phases. This pre-planning needs to account for the number of pages in each signature, based on both customer and equipment considerations. These considerations may include the total number of pages, the size of the stock to be printed, the press size, the number of feeder pockets available on the saddle-stitching equipment, and the number of inserts.

Imposition allowances need to be made for the lip, an extension on one side of the signature. The lip is gripped by mechanical "fingers" on the saddle stitcher to hold the signature open to its center spread for stitching. *Creep* (alternatively known as *push-out* or *thrust*) also needs to be considered during design and imposition.

Saddle Stitcher Components

The machines that perform saddle stitching are called wire stitchers, saddle

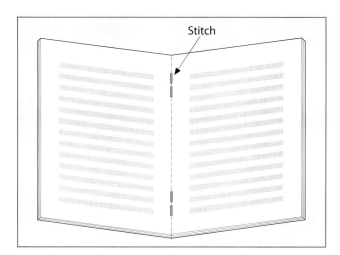
A saddle-stitched booklet.

Stitch

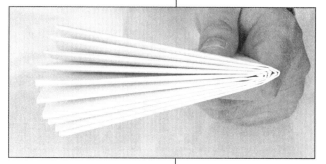
Creep, or push-out.

27

stitchers, or just stitchers. Stitchers range from small manually powered models to large automated machines.

Smaller saddle stitchers produce between ten thousand and twelve thousand units per hour; larger ones can handle as many as fourteen thousand units per hour. Saddle stitching is most effective for binding publications that are up to 0.25 in. (6 mm) thick. Thicker publications can require an awkwardly large creep allowance. This, in turn, increases the size of the printing stock and the resulting waste that must be trimmed off.

Saddle stitchers have three main segments: the pockets (signature feeding stations), the stitching heads, and three-knife trimmers. Collectively, these units are called an inserter/saddle stitcher/trimmer finishing line.

Pockets. Each folded signature is fed into the stitcher from a separate pocket. Mechanical "fingers" combined

With an automatic saddle-stitcher, the operator places signatures into hoppers, and then the signatures are automatically fed onto the conveyor.

with vacuum suction open each signature to its center before dropping it over the moving saddle-bar (sometimes called the *bayonet* or *sword*). A pin sweeps the first signature off the saddle-bar and pushes it toward the second pocket, where the next signature drops over it. This process continues until all of the signatures are stacked and the cover drops from the last pocket nearest the stitching heads.

Saddle stitchers are manufactured with different numbers of pockets. It takes five pockets, for example, to handle a four-signature publication with a cover. Pre-assembled inserts, subscription cards, and other advertisements can also be fed through the stitcher pockets and assembled with the signature pages. Compressed air is often used to "blow in" advertisement cards after the pages have been assembled but not yet stitched. A static charge or a small dab of adhesive holds the cards in place.

Magazines that are addressed parallel to the spine by inkjet or that have personalized inkjet messages pass through the inkjet station before stitching.

Stitching section. An operator-set caliper in the stitching section detects whether signatures or groups of signatures are thicker or thinner than the job thickness. Copies with missing signatures or with double-feeds go through without being stitched and are automatically ejected before reaching the trimmer. These signatures can be re-collated and run through the stitcher again.

Some stitchers have a control device on every feeding pocket to make sure that a signature has been fed. If it has not, all the following pockets are signaled so they do not drop their signatures onto the faulty copy. The faulty copy is ejected before it reaches the stitching section.

In the stitching section, a similar device makes sure that all books have the correct number of stitches. Copies with missing stitches are also delivered to a reject tray. Stitcher heads feed staples from continuous spools of wire. The gauge or thickness of the wire depends on the

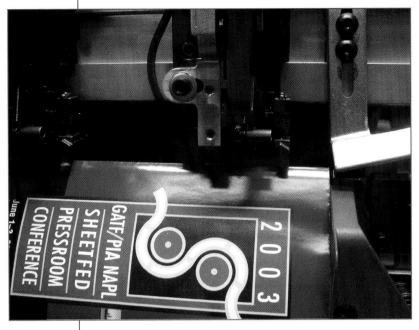

A close-up of the stitcher head on a saddle stitcher.

stitching machine and the thickness of the publication to be stapled. Clinching devices reach up through the signatures and bend the wire legs together to secure each staple. The depth of the legs is related to the length of the wire and can be adjusted to suit the thickness of the publication.

Trimming. Three-knife trimmers cut bound products to their final sizes. The trimmers slit open the folds on the front, head, and tail of the stitched signatures and cut away binding laps and any other excess, usually as part of an in-line operation. At the trimmer infeed, squeeze rollers remove trapped air and flatten the folds. The flattened unit, often called a *book block*, is then forwarded to the first trimming station. The untrimmed publication is held securely and squarely against the register stops, the

trim edge is clamped, and the front knife makes the first cut. The publication then goes to the head/foot trimming station. A conveyor usually carries the trimmed publications to the delivery table.

Some three-knife trimmers are designed to trim magazines, while others are used in the mass production of books. Five-knife trimmers may be used in high-volume operations to cut apart and trim two or more publications.

Modular Equipment and Accessories

Modular equipment and other accessories are often used to increase the versatility of saddle-stitch operations. Saddle-stitcher accessories may include the following:

- Take-off spinners (spools of wire secured to the floor behind the stitching section).
- Narrow stitching heads to bind two- and three-up jobs and very small booklets with stitches that are closer together.
- An oblique sheet monitor mounted between the last feeding pocket and the first stitcher. This quality control device detects unevenly jogged signatures and automatically diverts them, unstitched and untrimmed, into a reject tray for refeeding.
- In-line folder/feeder that automatically scores and folds cover stock and places it on the saddle-chain.
- Compensating counter/stacker that frees stitcher operators from manually counting, jogging, and stacking lifts of stitched and trimmed products at the delivery end of the saddle-stitching operation.
- Batch counters that collect the finished publications in predetermined lots (as few as five or as many as one hundred).

Batch counter.

29

- Tip-on/tip-in machines that secure inserts to saddle-stitched signatures with a thin strip of adhesive. These units also attach endpapers to adhesive-bound books. Reply cards, coupons, envelopes, and sample merchandise are among the items secured to the front and back pages of signatures.

- Automatic bundling units that compress stacks of signatures into more compact loads. Highly automated bundling systems compress signatures into 3-ft. (1-m) stacks called *logs*. The log form tightens the folds and protects the signatures from damage during handling.

- Multiple-hole punchers that use three- or five-hole dies to make holes along the spines of pamphlets and booklets after stitching and trimming.

- Chip disposal systems that use vacuum suction to filter trimmings and other debris away from the stitcher and through tubing hooked to a central disposal system or a scrap bin.

- Inkjet addressing units that place addresses in-line with the bottom of publications. These units can be placed after the trimmer on the saddle-stitching line.

- Automated postal sorting equipment that feeds labeled publications into a stacker according to ZIP Code groups. The stacked publications can be bundled, strapped, shrink-wrapped, and loaded onto pallets or placed directly into postal mailing sacks.

Top: Close-up of a conveyor chain.
Bottom: A conveyor chain in operation.

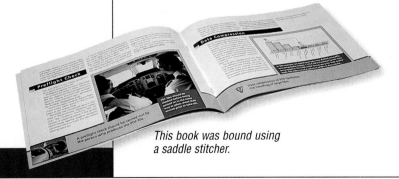

This book was bound using a saddle stitcher.

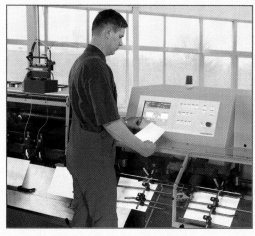

Representative of the saddle-stitching technology now being developed are the Heidelberg Stitchmaster ST 400 (top) and the Xerox SquareFold™ Booklet Maker (bottom left and right), both recipients of 2003 GATF InterTech Technology Awards.

The Booklet Maker is designed to meet the need for on-demand binding of jobs printed on digital presses. It produces a square-fold edge on saddle-stitched booklets, giving the look and feel of a perfect-bound book, including preprinted color covers with text on the spine. Based on technology designed by Plockmatic International AB, the unit connects in-line to Xerox DocuTech Production Publishers.

Operated via touch screen and a touch-sensitive keyboard (bottom left), the computer-driven Stitchmaster ST 400 has independent servo motors and mobile feeders equipped with wheels. The feeders can be moved around the shop floor so the feeder configuration can easily be changed. The Stitchmaster can be preset with local or network data, including prepress CIP data. It has an output of up to 14,000 cycles an hour and can handle products up to 12-5/8 by 19-7/8 inches.

Adhesive binding, one of the most popular methods of joining pages together, is more commonly referred to as *perfect binding*, and it is characterized by a spine that is flat and squared off. It takes practice—in operating the machinery, in project planning, and in client/printer/bindery communication—to make perfect binding "perfect." The difference between a successful perfect-binding job and a failure, for example, can be as small as a forgotten 1/8-in. grind-off margin.

What Is Adhesive (Perfect) Binding?

Adhesive binding gets its name because it uses a flexible glue to hold the pages of a publication together at its backbone. The thread-sewing method of bookbinding also uses an adhesive, but in true adhesive binding adhesive/glue is the only binding material.

Adhesive binding is used extensively to bind magazines, phone books, and the ever-popular paperback (or softcover) book. Perfect-bound magazines include such examples as *National Geographic* and *Reader's Digest*. Perfect binding is most often done as an in-line operation, especially for digital on-demand and personalized print jobs.

Examples of perfect-bound publications.

Adhesive binding offers several advantages:

- The squared backbone of the cover can be printed with the name of the publication or other information. This information can be read easily when the publication is stacked on a shelf.
- Like saddle stitching, books can be bound in one continuous operation from signatures to finished product.

- Single sheets and separate inserts can be added easily to perfect-bound publications. This makes it easy to produce different versions of the same magazine or catalog to send to different parts of a country or throughout the world.

Another form of adhesive binding is called *tape binding*. Tape binding gets its name from the fact that it uses a strip of flexible cloth tape containing a heat-activated glue that is applied to the edge of a stack of paper. The glue dries almost instantly as it cools and the finished pieces will lie flat when opened. This binding method is often seen on products that are produced quickly on-demand but need to be durable. Tape binding is usually an alternative to comb or coil binding, as it saves on the time and production costs involved in punching the documents to receive the mechanical bindings. In addition to being a bit more flexible and laying flatter than standard perfect binding, the tape also helps to reduce tearing of the spine with frequent use. Unlike the traditional perfect-binding methods described, the title cannot be printed on a tape-bound spine.

Adhesive-Binding Equipment

Perfect binding takes place in a finishing line consisting of a gatherer, backbone cutter and roughener,

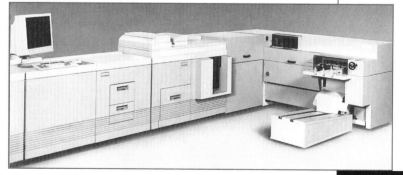

The Bourg Book Factory provides in-line capabilities to the Xerox DocuTech.

gluer, cover feeder, trimmers, and a counter stacker. The finishing line can be a standalone but continuous operation, and it can also be attached to a digital press.

Gatherer

Gatherers are devices with pockets (also called *hoppers*) for holding separate signatures, inserts, foldouts, etc., so they can be collected in the correct order for a publication. Gatherers may have a rotary, swinging arm, or planetary design (a system in which one part moves around another fixed or moving part) and anywhere from fewer than ten to more than thirty-two pockets. The pockets may be fed by hand or by an automatic system. Automated gatherers have sensors that report jams, misfeeds, or other interruptions. Incomplete piles are automatically rejected. The gathered group of signatures and inserts, etc., is called a *book block*.

Backbone Cutter and Roughener

In order for the adhesive binding material to work effectively, the signature folds at the spine (backbone) of the book block have to be removed before the glue is applied. This is the job of the backbone cutter and roughener.

At this stage, the gathered books blocks are carried, spine down, by clamps to the binding section. The part of the spine that extends out from the clamps is prepared to accept the glue in one of several ways:

- *Milling*, in which knives, saws, or shredders grind away the signature folds and then roughen the spine.
- *Notch binding*, in which large grooves are cut across the spine. The depth and spacing of the notches depends on the paper type and the composition of the adhesive.
- *Burst binding*, which features perforations in the creases of the signature folds. The perforations allow

the glue to penetrate, so it is not necessary to cut away the signature folds with this type of adhesive binding.

The stock used for printing is a factor in perfect binding, as is the printing itself. Papers with short fibers, dust particles from the milling process, and inks that are printed to bleed into the binding fold edge can interfere with glue adhesion.

Gluer

Still clamped together, the book block goes on to the gluing station, where applicator wheels apply the adhesive at a metered thickness. Some jobs need more than one application of more than one type of adhesive. With regular-sized paperback books, for example, a low-viscosity hot-melt glue is applied to hold the pages together. A high-viscosity hot-melt adhesive is used to attached the cover to the book block. Thick catalogs and telephone books may use three different types of adhesives.

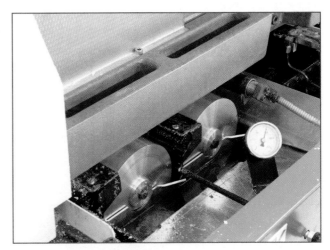

Close-up of a roller gluing unit.

Adhesives

Several types of adhesives are used in perfect binding: hot melt, polyvinyl acetate (PVA), and polyurethane-reactivate (PUR).

Hot-melt glues, which are used in traditional perfect binding, consist of polymers mixed with resins. They are relatively inexpensive and dry (or cure) by cooling. They form a strong bond under most conditions but do not hold up well under extreme temperatures. Hot-melt glues are most effective for binding periodicals, catalogs, and paperbacks. These glues require using a *premelter*, a separate piece of equipment that gradually and uniformly melts the glue. The premelter is attached to the gluing station on the perfect binder, and a pump releases the required amount of adhesive to the glue pot after the glue reaches a specified temperature. Repeated reheating weakens a hot-melt glue.

Polyvinyl acetate (PVA) adhesives are used in case binding as well as perfect binding catalogs and paperbacks. Applied cold, PVA glues provide a more flexible backbone than hot-melt glues but require a special oven to enhance drying. As it dries, the water in PVA glue evaporates and the solids polymerize (or cross-link) to form a strong bond. PVA resins penetrate deeply into the structure of the paper stock, forming a strong bond.

Polyurethane (PUR) adhesives are the newest adhesives used in binding. They yield products that lie flatter and require less backbone preparation than other adhesives. PURs, however, are more expensive, and the curing time is long and can be adversely affected by moisture from the paper stock and the surrounding air.

PUR adhesives also emit methylene biphenyl (a chemical combination similar to paint thinner) when heated. PUR glue pots need to be ventilated to prevent irritation of the eyes, mucous membranes, and skin.

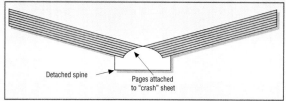

Detached spine — Pages attached to "crash" sheet

Top: A publication bound using the Otabind method.
Bottom: Lay-flat adhesive spine.

Lay-Flat Perfect Binding

Traditionally adhesive-bound publications do not lay completely flat. Several perfect binding options do, however, offer a lay-flat feature. The Otabind process, developed by Finland-based Otava Publishing Company, uses "two shots" of a cold-applied PVA glue down the spine of the book block to adhere pages to a crash paper liner. The cover is then glued to the side of the book block, rather than across the entire width of the spine as in traditional perfect binding. This, along with the use of the PVA glue provides the flexibility for the pages to "lay flat."

RepKover, licensed by Otabind, uses a cloth strip mounted on the inside of the spine to reinforce the soft cover of a book. It is frequently used for short runs as an alternative to Otabind. RepKover does involve extra production steps and specific types of equipment.

Some binderies use PUR hot-melt glue as a lay-flat adhesive option. The glue itself is more flexible than other types of glues. Just using this adhesive doesn't produce publications that lie as flat as either Otabind or RepKover.

Feeder guard.

Tip Sheet: Safety and Health

Safe practices are important in the perfect-binding line, where the equipment runs at high speeds, incorporates many revolving and cutting knives, and uses hot glues.

- Hit the safe button before making any adjustments to the binding line. The length of the line, especially when a three-knife trimmer is part of it, makes it difficult to see all of the workers.

- Handle rotary knives and rougheners with care. Remove the guards carefully before making any adjustments or repairs. Never touch a knife that is still moving. Newer machines have brakes that stop the knives and rougheners from rotating as soon as the power is cut off or guards are opened.

- Hot-melt glues reach 350–400°F (177–204°C) and can stick to everything—including flesh. Keep a bucket of water nearby to quickly cool a glue splash or spill and never load the gluing station manually. Use a separate hot-melt premelter for additional safety.

- Be cautious when crossing from one side of the machine to the other. Do not jump over conveyors or other moving machinery. The bindery may place bridges that employees can use for crossing.

- Use waste exhaust systems to minimize dust particles.

- Bale waste for reprocessing.

Cover Feeder

In a customary cover application for perfect-bound books, the cover falls from a hopper into a rotary or stream feeder, is scored from one to six times, then jogged for alignment before being pressed against the glue-covered backbone of the book block. Nipping stations pinch the cover around the spine, while clamps press the front, back, and sides against the book block. The bound book drops onto a conveyor belt to be sent to the trimmer.

Top: In-line cover feeder.

Bottom: Close-up of cover feeder assembly unit.

Trimmer

Once the adhesive is cool or cured enough for further processing, the tops of the folded signatures of the book block need to be trimmed to open them. Other trimming may also be needed. Although often done in-line, this can also be an offline operation. Trimming is usually done with three-knife or five-knife trimmers. Some binderies may use single-knife guillotine cutters.

A bindery can opt to trim two, three, or four books in the "collect mode" by placing one book on top of another (referred to as "two-on") and trimming them simultaneously. The collect mode is most useful when trimming thinner books. If a trimmer that normally cuts six thousand books per hour is set to deliver three books as one, it can output eighteen thousand books per hour.

Some binderies use dual trimmer lines to boost productivity. Trimmers can also be combined with counter/stackers, packing machines, and palletizers that prepare groups of finished products for shipment. The counter/stacker counts the number of units coming off the finishing line and stacks them for shipping.

Despite the Internet and the popularity of relatively inexpensive paperback books, we still use hardcover books—and lots of them—in schools, libraries, churches, and our homes (think of dictionaries, Bibles, and coffee table books). All of the major bookstores still stock more hardcover books than paperbacks. Hardcover books are also known as *casebound books* because of the name of the process (case binding) that is used to hold the pages together inside a cover (which is called a *case*).

What Is Case Binding?

Case binding, a time-tested binding style with its roots in hand binding, is at once elegant, durable, and practical. The process of case binding books, however, remains a mystery to most consumers—and even to many in the printing industry. Look at a paperback book, and a casual observer can easily see that making it somehow involves collected pages, a cover, and glue. Look at a

hardcover book, and it is not as easy to follow the many steps used to case bind it.

There are three types of case binding:

- *Edition binding*, which refers to the binding of hardcover books in large quantities.
- *Job binding*, which describes the binding of small quantities of hardcover books. It involves considerable handwork and is also used for books that cannot be handled by automatic equipment (e.g., books bound in soft leather).
- *Library binding*, which refers to special services for libraries, such as pre-binding, rebinding, and repair work.

This chapter puts a magnifying glass on the steps involved in edition binding. Although the steps are explained separately, in-line equipment for high-volume edition binding combines operations (e.g., forwarding and covering operations, including rounding, backing,

A large edition bindery may have many types of equipment and machines, including:

- Blocking presses
- Board cutters
- Book jacketing machines
- Bundling presses
- Case-making machines
- Casing-in machines
- Cloth-slitting machines
- Cutter-perforating machines
- Endpaper-signature stripping machines
- Endpaper tipping machines
- Folding machines
- Gathering machines
- Gluing-off machines
- Nipping presses
- Rounding and backing machines
- Saddle-stitching machines
- Sewing machines
- Three-knife (or five-knife) trimmers
- Tipping machines
- Triple liner and headbanding machines
- Wrapping machines (book jacketing machines)

This list comes from the entry for "edition binding" in the online version of *Bookbinding and the Conservation of Books: A Dictionary of Descriptive Terminology* by Matt T. Roberts and Don Etherington. The dictionary is comprehensive and easily searchable. At publication time, it could be found under http://palimpsest.stanford.edu/don/don.html.

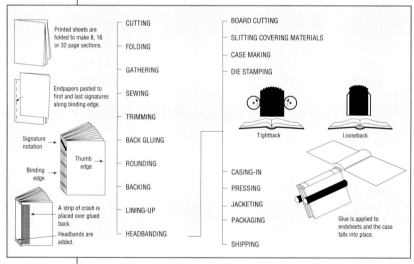

Casebinding.

casing-in, building-in, and jacketing) into one automated production line.

Folding

Folding, which can be either a presswork or bindery operation, is covered in its own chapter. It is, however, a first step in case binding because it is necessary to create the signatures that make up the inside of the book. The press size and type, paper thickness, and other considerations determine what kind of signatures are printed and sent to the bindery and whether they arrive folded or unfolded.

Large press sheets are folded to produce signatures of 8, 12, 16, 24, 32, or 48 pages. Four-page signatures are generally not recommended for case binding because the thread sewing will rip through the single folded edge of the paper. If a four-page signature is necessary, it may be tipped (glued) to or inserted inside another signature, preferably in the middle of the book.

Gluing (Tipping) Endsheets

The endsheet, also called an *endpaper* or *endleaf*, is what readers see immediately inside the cover when they open the front or back cover of a book. These sheets, either blank or decorated, are cut, folded, then glued (tipped) to the first and last signatures of a book before the signatures are gathered together. They are eventually glued to the case, or cover, boards to hold the book together.

Gathering

Gathering is the process of collecting all of the signatures that make up a book in the correct order. The gathered signatures are called *book blocks*. In edition binding operations, gathering is an automated process done by machine. Gathering machines use one of three different designs: swinging arm, rotary drum, or planetary. All have pockets, or hoppers, into which the signatures are fed either manually or automatically.

Mechanical devices called *calipers* are used to detect if a signature is omitted or if two signatures from a pocket are deposited onto the gathered signatures. Electronic sensors, bar coding, and other identification steps may also be used to make sure that all of the signatures are gathered and that they are in the correct order. If there is a problem, the machine automatically stops, identifies the problem pocket, and sends the faulty book block to a reject area.

Thread Sewing

After gathering, the signatures are sewn both separately and to other signatures using machine thread sewing. Thread sewing for case binding is divided into two categories similar to wire stitching: side sewing and saddle sewing (also called Smyth sewing).

Side sewing, used mostly for library binding and repair work, links signatures by passing a thread through

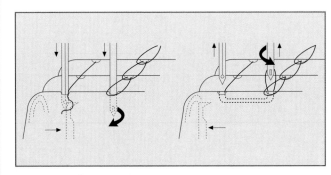

Diagram of Smyth sewing process.

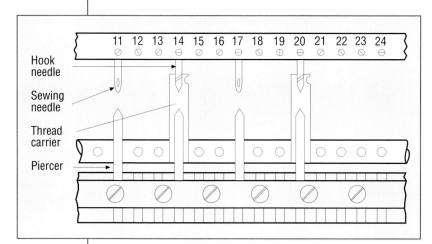

Units in thread sewing.

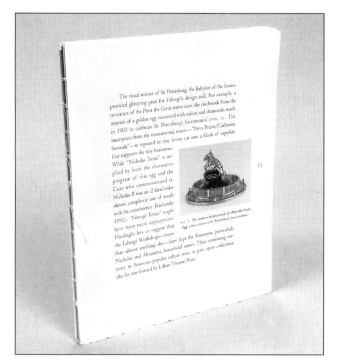

A sewn book block.

the side of the binding edge. It can be done by hand or by machines that run the thread through drilled holes. This binding is strong, but the pages do not lie flat when the book is opened.

Smyth sewing passes the thread through the back fold of a signature and then goes from signature to signature. It links the signatures and produces a book whose pages lie flat when the book is opened.

Machine saddle sewing is done with a series of needles. It can be done by passing the thread through just the signature folds or also through spine lining material or tape. Some machines are designed to pass the thread around the tape instead of through it.

Book sewing threads include linen (with a glazed finish), cotton, nylon, terylene, and a combination of cotton and terylene.

Saddle sewing uses one of four basic lockstitch patterns: standard, continuous, staggered, and continuous staggered.

The *standard* and *continuous lockstitch* patterns always place the stitch in the same place in each signature. This produces a buildup of thread that can make the spine thicker than the rest of the book block, especially on book blocks with few pages. *Nipping* or *smashing* will compress the spine edge expanded by the stitches. A *staggered* pattern places the stitches in alternate signatures and cuts the thread buildup in half. *Continuous staggered* stitches make solid diagonal lines across the spine and produce a secure binding.

Nipping and Smashing

As mentioned, book blocks are either nipped or smashed to reduce the thickening effects of thread buildup on the spine. Nipping applies pressure only along the sides of the backbone. Smashing applies pressure over

Principles of nipping (top) and smashing (bottom).

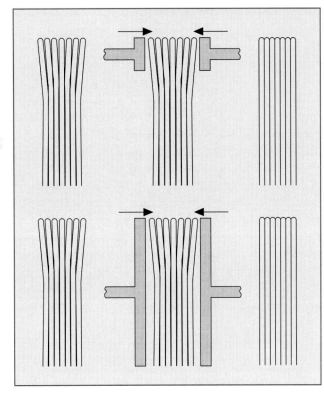

stitches from pulling apart and puts the block in the proper flexible condition for rounding and backing.

Trimming

At this point, most book blocks are ready for trimming, which is done on three-knife or five-knife trimmers. Trimming opens any closed folds along the edges of the book block and reduces the blocks to the desired trim size. After trimming, the book blocks move through a series of book block finishing steps called *forwarding*.

Forwarding

Forwarding includes both essential operations and optional decorative steps.

Rounding/backing. Rounding curves the spine of the book block to better fit the cover. A round-backed book is first rounded, then backed using a machine called a *rounding and backing machine* or a *forwarding machine*. Rollers give the book block a convex (outward curving) spine and a concave (inward curving) front edge. A *backing iron* flares the spine, making it wider than the thickness of the rest of the book. This creates "shoulders" that help keep the front and back covers

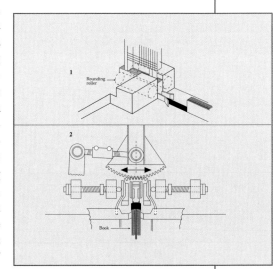

Diagram of a rounding and backing machine and a book placed between the rounding rollers.

the entire front and back of the book block, which also removes excess air from the book block. Smashing is important in edition binding because it makes all the book blocks uniformly thick so that the machines (e.g., rounding and backing, casing-in, etc.) can be set up just once for the entire run of the edition.

Gluing

In addition to thread sewing, an adhesive or a glue is applied to the spine of the book block. This keeps the

42

in place and hinge creases that help the book to be opened.

Back lining or spine lining. One or several layers of cloth, paper, or a glue or a flexible resin are applied to the spine by a special machine in whatever combination has been chosen. This step reinforces the sewn backbone and helps maintain the spine's rounded shape. This step is important to the overall strength and durability of the finished book.

Book blocks are attached to the case inside the front and back covers, but not at the spine. Gluing only the end-sheets to the inside of the case boards is not enough to keep the two securely attached. The remedy is to glue a strong piece of cloth to the spine when back lining is done. The cloth is wider than the spine of the book and is glued to the case boards underneath and along with the end-sheets.

Headbanding. Head and tail bands are ornamental strips of reinforced cotton or silk that are attached to the top and bottom of the backbone of book blocks. In edition binding, headbanding is done during back/spine lining by the same machine.

Edge treatment. In this optional decoration operation, the edges of books are stained with decorative colorings or coated with gold leaf.

Casemaking

Making the case, or the cover, of the book is a separate operation. It can be done at the same time that the signatures are being gathered and sewn or at another time.

Cases are made of a heavy inner material, called *board*, which is covered by an outside layer of printed paper, cloth, or some other material. The board is slit into strips, then cut to the right size before being fed into the casemaking machine along with the outside cover material. The outside cover material can come in rolls or in sheets cut to the right size.

The casemaking machine "glues off" the cover material, places the boards and spine on it, then wraps the flaps of extra cover material around the boards, forming a finished edge. Covers may be stamped or embossed at this

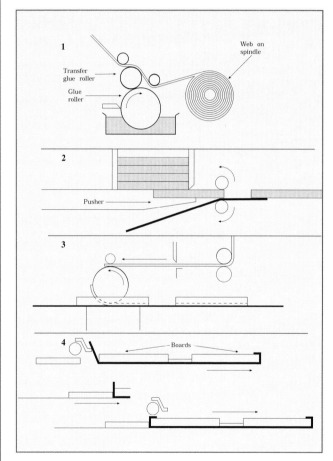

Steps in auto casemaking.

43

time. After this, the case is ready to be attached to the book block.

Attaching the Case

Attaching the finished case to the book blocks involves two operations:

- *Casing-in* attaches the cover to the book by gluing the cover to the endsheets and any reinforcement strips glued to the spine earlier. This is done by a semiautomatic or automatic casing-in machines. The book blocks are hung from their centers over a metal "wing." The machine then clamps the book, coats the endpapers with adhesive, fits the case on the text block, and completes the operation.

- *Building-in* refers to drying the case adhesive under pressure. Building-in machines substitute heat and great pressure for the element of time required to set and cure the cover adhesive and form the joints. The machines, which can be fed manually or automatically, use a series of pressure plates and heated joint formers. Each set of plates and joint formers clamps the book under great pressure for a moment and then releases it. A book may pass through five or more sets of clamps and formers, depending on the amount of drying needed.

Book Jacketing

Books jackets, or the outside cover wrap, were originally used to protect the covering material of the book from dirt or other damage. Now, book jackets are also used for promotional purposes. Modern book jackets are often elaborately designed, use decorative features like embossing and metallic inks, and are printed in color, and as such are frequently produced by specialty printers.

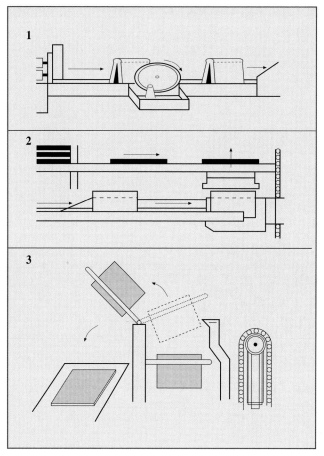

Steps in auto casing-in.

Usually detachable, book jackets are flush with the covers of the book at head and tail but are folded over the fore edge of both covers. Book jackets are also called book wrappers, dust covers, dust jackets, dust wrappers, jackets, and wrappers. Book jacketing can be done by hand, or it can be part of an automated, in-line production operation.

The pages of many business and presentation publications—and all those calendars and organizers and so many regional cookbooks—might be left at loose ends were it not for mechanical binding and ring binding.

What Is Mechanical Binding?

A variety of mechanical-bound publications.

The mechanical binding process uses coiled or looped plastic or wire to hold pages and covers together. The process is fairly simple, requiring only hole punching for the internal pages and the cover, then collating and binding. Mechanical binding has become a highly automated operation. Popular mechanical binding methods include spiral binding, twin-loop wire binding, and plastic comb binding.

Spiral binding. A spring-like coil of plastic or wire is wound through small holes drilled in one edge of the collated sheets and cover to make a book or booklet. Each end of the coil is cut and bent or "crimped" to keep the coil and pages from unwinding. This is a one-time binding method, and the books cannot be re-opened to add or change pages.

Twin-loop wire binding. The pages and cover of the book are hooked onto looped, pre-opened wire "teeth," and then the arrangement is closed. This binding method, also a one-time binding method, is sometimes referred to as Wire-O® binding.

Plastic comb binding. The binding machine holds open a plastic tube with comblike fingers, and the drilled, collated publication is fitted over the comb. When released, the fingers close, keeping the pages together. This is a cost-effective binding for short runs with little setup, and the books can be re-opened and pages can be removed or added. It is sometimes called GBC (General Binding Corporation) binding.

Ring and post binding. Ring and post binding remain popular despite developments in wire stitching, adhesives, and in-line binding. Ring and post binding are easy, well-known, and inexpensive, and they let creators and users insert and delete pages at will. Many business publications and printed training or procedure manuals are ring bound, also referred to as binders. Post binding is often found in libraries, holding together the various issues of one volume of a magazine, for instance. The posts in this method are similar to a screw and nut; one post screws into the other through opposite ends of the hole punched through the printed material, holding them securely together.

Planning

Mechanical and loose-leaf bindings may seem elementary, but just as with other binding and finishing operations, planning and design can make the difference between products that serve their purpose well and those that do not.

If a book has critical crossovers (e.g., maps, artwork, or diagrams) at a spread, the Wire-O and GBC styles can be the better choice because they open without stepping up or down. If a book is to be held in one hand, like an

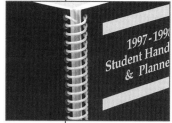

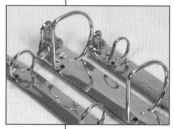

From top to bottom, examples of mechanical binding methods: spiral-bound using plastic coil, semi-concealed Wire-O® binding, plastic comb binding (GBC), and ring bindings.

Example of crossover.

equipment manual or some maps, a binding style that opens 360 degrees might be the best choice. If the books will be exposed to extreme temperatures, remember that plastic bindings can melt or crack.

Drilling also needs to be planned so the holes don't go through essential information. Planning can also increase bindery efficiency. For example, it might be best to lay out a 4×6-in. (101.6×152.4 mm) oblong job to be punched on the 4-in. side as two-up for automatic punching, especially if this eliminates hand feeding lifts into a manual punching machine.

As it affects hole punching, grain direction can be important with a heavier stock. And what needs to be done first on which machine also needs to be considered. For example, one bindery may find it best to fold and cut a job; another may find it more efficient and economical to cut and collate it.

According to the online version of *The Columbia Guide to Standard American English,* published on www.bartleby.com, "to take stock of something" is to survey it carefully… "We must take stock of our situation" means "We must carefully examine and consider it." This chapter takes stock of the central and most important stock used in printing (and therefore in the bindery)—paper.

Paper Considerations

How well a job reproduces on press and then withstands cutting, folding, perforating, gluing, or other binding and finishing processes depends partly on the material it is printed on—the substrate, or the stock. The stock can be a form of board or plastic, a metal, or any other material that the printing press can handle. Paper, however, remains the stock of choice and the central material for printing. It is available in hundreds of types and basis weights—and it may also account for about 30% to 50% of the total cost of commercial printing jobs.

The more bindery workers know about the major material they handle every day, the better they can take stock of bindery operations and troubleshoot problems. A bindery worker who understands paper properties will be able to adjust a binding or finishing machine, or an operation, to accommodate the paper.

Paper Properties

Of all the properties (physical, optical, chemical) connected with paper, the following are most important to binding and finishing operations: caliper, grain, dimensional stability, density, smoothness.

Caliper

Caliper refers to the thickness of a paper. It is measured in thousandths of an inch (e.g., 0.004 in.) or in points, with one point equal to one thousandth of an inch (0.001 in.). In the metric system, caliper (also called micrometer) is measured in millimeters and micrometers. Caliper is measured using an instrument called a *micrometer.* Some bindery machines, for example folders and signature gatherers, are adjusted according to the caliper measure of a paper, a signature, or a group of signatures.

Grain

Grain refers to the alignment of the fibers in the paper. This alignment occurs because of the way paper is manufactured, and it affects paper in several ways.

- Paper tears and folds more easily in the grain direction than across it.
- Paper curls following the grain direction.

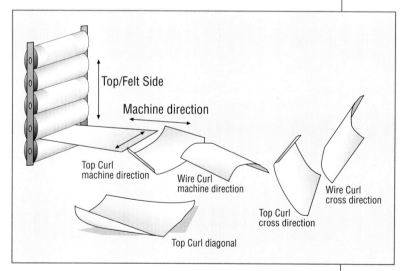

A variety of ways paper can curl as a result of grain direction.

- Paper shows greater stiffness and strength against the grain.
- With changes in moisture content, paper changes more in the direction going across the grain than with the grain.

The effects of grain direction on bindery operations can be both negative and positive. Folds made parallel to (with) the grain are neater and more resilient. Folds made perpendicular to (against) the grain may not lay as flat, and the fold edges can crack, especially if there is heavy or solid ink coverage.

Print jobs that will be bound are usually planned so the grain direction runs parallel to the binding edge. This can prevent buckling and cracking at the spine and makes the pages less stiff in the turning direction.

When printing a heavy basis weight paper, a sheetfed press operator might need to print using a grain direction favorable to presswork. This might conflict with folding or binding requirements. The printer and binder need to decide in advance what compromise to make.

Grain Property	In the grain direction	Across direction
Tear strength is generally	—	Greater
Tensile strength is always	Greater	—
Stretch under tension is always	—	Greater
Folding endurance is generally	—	Greater
Paper folds	More easily, with less tendency to crack	—
Tensile strength at fold is	—	Greater
Stiffness and resistance to bending is always	—	Greater
Expansion or contraction with change in relative humidity is always	—	Greater

Effect of grain direction on paper properties.

Dimensional Stability

Dimensional stability refers to how well paper holds its size when the temperature and moisture content, of both the surrounding environment and the paper itself, change.

Most people are surprised to find out how sensitive paper is to temperature and moisture. Paper fibers have considerable ability to gain or lose moisture. Because of this characteristic, paper expands or contracts more than enough to cause registration problems in the pressroom and edge distortion and other problems for the bindery. Paper will change dimension as it moves through the lithographic printing process because the process itself transfers moisture to the paper; dryers at the end of a web press remove moisture. Pages or covers cut to precise dimensions the day before can seem to mysteriously lengthen or shorten overnight so that one no longer matches the other. Once perfectly flat pages can become wavy, and bindings can detach. Paper that would have been foldable may suddenly seem too "thick" for a folder to handle.

Moisture loss from a pile of paper can cause the edges to shrink but leave the inner area unaffected. In this case, the paper is described as "tight edged." When a pile of paper absorbs moisture at its exposed edges, the edges expand and become wavy. The edge that is across the grain will be wavier than the edge parallel to the grain.

Several practices can help prevent moisture-related paper problems:

- **Proper storage in warehouses and storage areas, pressrooms—and the bindery.** Proper storage means keeping paper in its original (and undamaged) wrappings as much as possible and then rewrapping it as needed between print production operations. Paper should never be stored in direct contact with concrete or damp floors; next to cold walls,

Paper and Grain Direction

As mentioned earlier in the text, folds made parallel to the grain are neater and more resilient, while folds made against the grain may not lay as flat. Likewise, when folding against the grain, the fold edges can crack, especially if there is heavy or solid ink coverage where the fold is planned. Paper grain and its relationship to stiffness are also important for many end-use requirements. For example, a print job to be bound should be planned so the grain direction runs parallel to the binding edge. Otherwise, the paper will tend to buckle and crack at the spine, and the pages will be stiffer and more difficult to turn. For display cards, file folders, and index cards, the grain direction should be at right angles to the supporting edge to minimize sagging.

When printing a heavy basis weight paper, a sheetfed press operator might need to print using a grain direction favorable to presswork. This might conflict with folding or binding requirements. It is up to the printer and binder to decide in advance what compromise to make.

Note: There are several ways to determine a paper's grain direction: (1) Float a sample on water or dampen it on one side; the grain will be parallel to the curl. (2) Tear a sample lengthwise, then crosswise. The tear with the grain will be relatively straight; the tear across the grain will be jagged and rough. (3) Pinch the fingernails of your thumb and middle finger around the edge of a piece of paper and slide them down one edge and then another edge perpendicular to the first one. With the grain, there will be almost no change; the edge against the grain will be clearly wavy. (4) Cut two long, thin strips at right angles to each other from the same sheet. Put one strip on top of another, and hold them together at one short edge. Let them dangle, then turn them both over and let them dangle again. When it is on the bottom, the short-grain strip will bend toward the ground more than the long grain strip. Or you can just hold each strip separately; the short-grain piece will bend more than the long-grain piece.

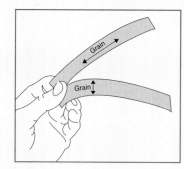

Flex test for determining grain direction. Paper cut in the direction of the paper grain (top) and across it. Paper is stiffer in the direction of the grain than across the grain, and folds are cleanest when made parallel to the grain direction.

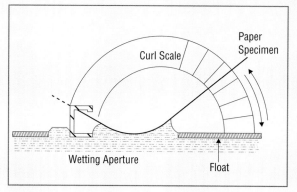

The curl test method for measuring a paper's water resistance.

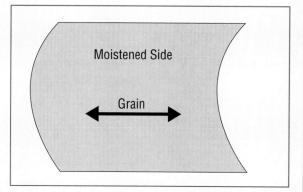

Curl test for determining grain direction.

At 50% relative humidity and 75°F (24°C), a 1,000-lb. (450-kg) load of sheets will contain as much as 8.4 gal. (31.8 l) of water, depending upon the composition of the paper.

At 10% relative humidity and 75°F (24°C), a 1,000-lb. (450-kg) load of sheets will contain only 3.6 gal. (13.6 l) of water.

heating devices, or vents; or in areas that have sudden and drastic temperature changes.

- **Temperature conditioning.** This means bringing the paper to pressroom or bindery temperature and relative humidity before working on it. Paper that is in relative balance with its surrounding atmosphere usually remains dimensionally stable.
- **Maintaining relative humidity (RH) in the pressroom and the bindery.** Paper made in the United States and Canada is manufactured for a relative humidity between 35% and 50%.

Density

Density refers to the weight of a paper related to how much paper there is in a certain unit. A four-inch stack of a dense paper, for example, weighs more than a four-inch stack of lower density paper. A bindery worker may need to cut smaller piles of high-density

paper or adjust the knife angle for a soft, low-density paper.

Smoothness and Texture

Smoothness is the measure of the evenness or lack of contour of a paper's surface. Smoother papers are considered to have better printability than less smooth papers. Smoothness can affect bindery operations, especially when the paper is not smooth but textured. Successful foil stamping, for example, requires a smooth surface. Smoothness can also affect paper stacking and feeding. Low-smoothness paper has less of a tendency to slip and slide, but too much texture and the paper may jam or slow some bindery operations. Smoothness can be measured in the laboratory with testing devices.

Choosing a Paper

The choice of the paper for a print job particularly illustrates how one part of the print production process affects others. Design and aesthetics are not the only reasons for choosing a paper for a print job. Bindery, mailing, and end use need to be considered as well.

Following are some print production considerations, not necessarily in order of their importance, that can affect paper choice at different stages of print production:

- End-use requirements, e.g., annual report, textbook, stand-up point-of-purchase display, label, envelope, greeting card, playing card, telephone directory, etc.
- Type and size of the press.
- Runnability, the physical ability of the paper to withstand the the mechanics of the pressrun.
- Printability, the extent to which paper properties lend themselves to reproducing something in print, e.g., whiteness, brightness, smoothness, opacity.

Point-of-purchase (POP) displays require a heavier, stiffer choice of paper stock.

- Gluability, which determines the speed and strength of a bond created by applying an adhesive. This is an issue in binding books and other publications and in making packaging. Sometimes a glue is not meant to be permanent but to release easily when it substitutes for wafer sealing or is used to keep gatefolds and foldouts from unraveling during binding.
- Grain direction of the fibers in sheets or rolls of paper.
- Size and number of pages to be printed on the form.
- Maximum sheet size that an in-line folder at the end of a web press or the bindery's folder can accept.
- Basis weight, the weight in pounds of a ream (500 sheets) of paper cut to a basic size. If 500 sheets of a 25×38-in. (635×965.2 mm) book paper weigh 70 lb., then the basis weight of that paper is 70 lb. In the metric system used outside the U.S., basis weight is referred to as *grammage* and is measured in grams per square meter. Grammage is not connected with a basic size of paper. Basis weight is important in determining the number of folds per signature. Lighter papers can accommodate more folds than heavier papers. Very light paper, like Bible paper, needs special equipment and experienced workers to guide it through the folder.

- Foldability, the number of double folds a paper will withstand before breaking under tension. The folding endurance of different papers ranges widely but is generally greater when the sheet is folded against the grain. Folding endurance is a good indicator of a paper's permanence and durability. When the bindery receives a job with numerous folds (e.g., maps, charts, and even covers and envelopes), it is important to test the stock's ability to withstand repeated folding and handling.

With a term like "finishing" used to describe a whole host of processes, how do we know when the project really is being finished? We may have to ask: "Is it finally what it is supposed to be?" It's an appropriate question for this chapter on finishing.

This chapter considers finishing from two catchall points of view:

- It takes into account that increasingly automated in-line and one-pass near-line and offline operations—plus the unique finishing needs connected with digital and personalized printing—have made it more difficult to say exactly when "finishing" (meaning all post-printing operations) begins and ends. Many times, especially with web and digital presswork, what were once completely offline and even separate finishing processes have crossed over to become part of the pressrun, part of units or cells of continuous work, part of mailing and distribution operations, or even part of a complete one-pass print job workflow.
- It considers finishing in its narrower definition as "specialty," "decorative," or "graphic" finishing rather than its encompassing definition as all post-printing operations.

When Is It Finishing?

Coatings provide one example of why it can be difficult to say exactly when something is part of the finishing process. Coatings, even ultraviolet-cured (UV) coatings, are now often applied as part of presswork. (Varnish, which is similar in formula to ink but without pigment, has always been applied on press.) So while "coating" may traditionally have been, and still is, categorized as "finishing,"

it isn't always done in the bindery or even as a separate finishing operation.

Inkjet addressing is another example. Inkjetting, which can now be done using an attachment on a saddle-stitch binder, blurs the line between binding and mailing/distribution. Some highly sophisticated printing operations aim to print and finish jobs in a complete, one-pass workflow connected to the press. At the end of the "pressrun," the printed product is ready to ship and mail.

Binding and finishing operations are not being eliminated. Cutting, folding, gathering, stitching, binding, etc., still need to be done. It all depends on

- How automated or manual the operations are
- Who does them (printer, trade binder, combination)
- Where/when they are done (pressroom or bindery, completely or partly in-line, offline, or near-line)

In-line, Offline, and Near-line

In-line finishing covers any finishing job completed on a sheetfed, web, or digital press that eliminates a subsequent bindery operation. The most highly developed and sophisticated in-line finishing is currently found with web press operations.

Besides using rotary cutters to separate the roll of paper into "ribbons" of different widths, web presses with in-line finishing machinery can sheet the ribbons and fold the sheets into signatures. Other in-line operations that can be done at the end of a web pressrun include the following:

- Contour and window diecutting
- Embossing and debossing
- Continuous and/or curved running-perforation segments

- Cross-web perforating
- Four-side bleed trims for flat sheets
- Backbone box scores
- Inserting
- Applying polyscents; scent strips; scratch-offs; rub-offs; microencapsulated fragrances; and remoistenable, wet-flap, spine, and spot glues

In-line web finishing is a popular way to produce direct-mail advertisements, advertising inserts for newspapers and magazines, lottery tickets and game pieces, promotional stamps, and envelopes.

Offline finishing refers to finishing done separately from printing, often in separate steps, and even in a totally different location. Even with offline finishing, however, the trend is to combine operations, e.g., folding and gluing, when possible.

Near-line finishing, the latest trend, puts both finishing operations and finishing systems close at hand, although not directly connected to the press. A near-line approach is often based on linking self-contained operations in one line.

Advertising inserts.

Digital Presses, Print On-Demand, and the Printrun of One

Unless the printed pieces are one-page flyers that will be placed, for example, under auto windshield wipers, jobs that are printed on digital presses also need to be "finished." Integrating finishing with digital printing presses is an especially active area of development. As with other types of printing and presses, finishing after digital or on-demand printing can be done in-line, offline, or near-line.

In one sense the required binding and finishing operations are the same: trimming, folding, gathering, wire stitching, perfect binding, and case binding. The nature of digital printing, however, offers some challenges to traditional binding and finishing machinery and practices.

Binderies that provide postpress services for digital printing may face challenges in handling toner-printed and odd-size stock on traditional equipment. Or it may not be cost-effective to use high-volume bindery machinery to handle short-run jobs (150 to 1,500 pieces). Not all digital print jobs are short-run jobs, however.

The turnaround time expected of digital printing also brings its own urgency to the concept of "Is it finished yet?" Print customers who expect digital printing "on demand" expect binding and finishing to be done on demand. Then, too, with personalized pieces, one-to-one marketing, and books/booklets printed in a quantity of one, there is no margin for binding and finishing errors. Ruining one piece ruins the entire printrun—a printrun of one—and requires reprinting.

More binding and finishing machinery for output from digital presses is being developed. Most of this machinery is as computerized and as automated as possible and designed to need as few operators and as little operator intervention as possible. It is also designed for in-line operations or some version of a single-pass near-line operation with a print-to-mail workflow in mind. Some examples include perfect binders, on-demand stitching machines, and even short-run case binding systems for books.

Graphic (Specialty or Decorative) Finishing: Catchall Basics

Graphic finishing is also called *specialty* or *decorative finishing* because it is done to enhance an already printed product. The most frequently encountered graphic finishing operations include, among others, coating, diecutting, embossing, foil stamping, gluing, inkjet addressing and personalization, and laminating.

Coating

Coating can be considered both an in-line presswork process as well as a form of off-press finishing. Coatings are used to create visual effects and to seal inks and prevent rub-off or abrasion. Four different press coatings are used in commercial printing: varnishes, aqueous coating, and ultraviolet (UV) and electron beam (EB) coating. All are available in matte, dull, and gloss formulations.

Varnish is a petroleum-based sealant essentially equivalent to printing ink but lacking a pigment. It is always applied by a standard inking unit on the press. It can be applied on the entire press sheet or in selected areas. Varnish is applied on the last unit, or as a second pass, to seal the offset inks and provide rub protection.

Aqueous coating, a water-based sealant, is applied by an inking unit on the press or by a special coater tower attached to the press.

Ultraviolet (UV) coating is a reactive, cross-linking system in which the vehicle is dried by exposure to UV radiation. UV coating may be applied as a separate finishing operation as a flood coating or (applied by screen printing) as a spot coating. It is a relatively thick coating that may crack when scored or folded in finishing operations.

Electron beam (EB) coatings share many of the same properties as UV coatings, such as quick drying times, high gloss, and abrasion resistance. The EB process, using the high energy level of accelerated electrons for the cross-linking process, produces a higher degree of conversion than does the lower energy UV process. This distinction makes EB coatings ideal for the food packaging industry as they emit only low levels of odors or other extractions.

Diecutting

Diecutting is a means of cutting designed shapes into preprinted stock. Most diecutting is done in the folding carton or paperboard industry, and it is used to create pop-up books and games and to cut flat printed stock into package or box shapes that will be assembled later. Diecutting is also used on greeting cards and advertising materials. This specialty operation is often done outside the bindery but may be combined with other bindery operations, for example, coating and gluing.

A variety of diecut products.

> **Tip Sheet:** It is not possible to inkjet, glue, or foil stamp over coatings. These operations need an uncoated window, or coating needs to be the final finishing step on a printed piece.

55

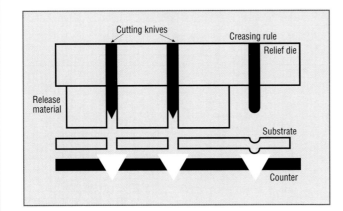

Principles of diecutting.

Examples of products that have been embossed.

Diecutting is done on flatbed platen presses, cylinder presses, hand-press diecutters, high-die label cutters, and on in-line rotary systems. Rotary high-die systems use a steel knife die for long production runs of labels and tags and for high-volume consumer items like milk cartons and paper cups and containers. Cardboard point-of-purchase (POP) displays are also shaped by steel-rule diecutters. Almost all in-line diecutting is done in accompaniment with flexographic or gravure presses.

Embossing

Embossing creates raised, or relief, images in stock. It is done on platen presses or other machinery that presses stock between a die and a counter-embossing form (a sunken die into which the relief die fits exactly). Embossing more commonly uses heated dies, but it can also be done with cold dies.

While separate machinery is available for embossing, foil stamping, and diecutting operations, these operations are often done on a single press.

Embossing that simply creates a raised image with no accompanying coloration (e.g., foil) or print is called *blind embossing*. Registration of all the print and emboss-

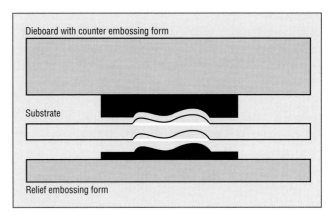

Typical embossing configuration.

ing elements is important, and misregistered embossing may well result in a totally unusable product. Embossing that is combined with foil stamping is called *foil embossing*. *Debossing* dies produce images that are depressed (sunken) into the surface of the stock. Debossed designs may also be blind or ornamental.

One of the most important elements in the embossing process (and foil stamping as well) is the die that is used to create the image or shape. Dies are usually made of magnesium, copper, or brass, depending on the complexity of the design, the material, and the run length of the job. Magnesium dies are used for shorter runs and uncomplicated designs. Brass dies are used for longer runs and complex designs. Dies can be single-level or multi-level with several distinct depths. The image in the die can be chemically etched, machine-cut, or hand-tooled. Dies are increasingly being manufactured by software-based laser systems.

Hot Foil Stamping

Hot foil stamping equipment uses a heated die and a thin film (foil) that contains metals or a pigment to put a decorative design on a material. The die is heated and pressed against the foil, which sits on top of the stock to be imprinted. The heat releases the coloring layer from the foil and binds it to the end product. Foil stamping is usually associated with metallic finishes like gold and silver. Stamping foil, however, is available in a wide range of colors, finishes, and effects, from marble, snakeskin, imitation leather, pearl, wood grain, and geometric patterns to holograms, pigments, metallics, and subtle tints, in matte and gloss finishes.

Hot foil stamping is also known as flat stamping, foil stamping, hot stamping, gold stamping, blocking, and leafing. It is a popular finishing technique because nearly anything that can withstand heat and pressure can be foil stamped. Foil-stamped images are added to promotional mailers, brochures, invitations, cloth book covers, wrapping paper, packaging, menus, and even children's books.

Hot foil stamping does not produce raised images, but it is often combined with embossing, which does produce raised images. This combination of work is called *foil embossing.*

Different foils have different durability characteristics (e.g., scratch, fade, and chemical resistance; brittleness; opacity; adherence). These characteristics, the

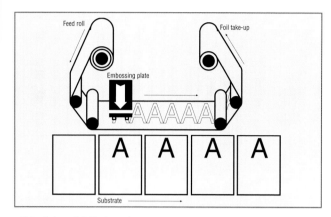

Principles of foil stamping.

Examples of foil-stamped products.

qualities of the selected stock, the depth and complexity of the artwork and dies, and the ink are all key elements in the success of a foil-stamped product.

You may have noticed some overlap among diecutting, foil stamping, and embossing; as mentioned earlier, these three processes can all be done on a single press and often are.

Gluing

Modern glues and gluing systems have widened the already large role that these elements play in print production and finishing. Gluing is no longer the frequently troublesome "specialty" that not too many years ago required extensive makeready and extremely skilled operators.

As a print production and finishing process, gluing has attached itself to other operations. In-line systems on web presses apply remoistenable glues for lick-and-stick envelopes; wet-flap glues to form envelope pockets on brochures; spine glues for catalogs and magazines; and spot glues for inserts and gatefolded materials for magazines, catalogs, and brochures. Gluing forms the backbone, literally, of perfect binding operations. Gluing can also be part of mailing and distribution operations, and it is certainly a huge factor in converting, an area not covered in this primer. Particularly in binderies, gluing systems are being attached to folders and used to apply adhesive to mailings, brochures, multi-page booklets, and other commercial products.

Apart from adhesive- and case-binding work, three major types of glues are used in print finishing: fugitive, remoistenable, and permanent. Remoistenable glue is usually applied in-line on a web press, but all of these glues can be applied in a bindery. Depending on the stock, the glue, and the reason for gluing, they can be applied cold or hot using a large number of devices and configurations. Gluing systems can have tanks, hoses,

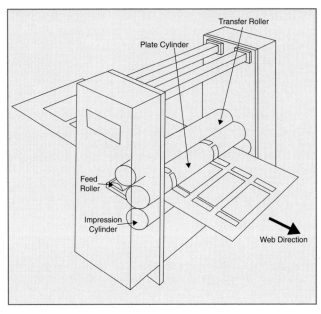

Remoistenable pattern gluer.

guns that spray or extrude glue, or rotating wheels and rollers.

Fugitive glue, also known as *easy-release* or *removable glue*, is designed to be detachable without tearing paper fiber and to be easily rubbed away after use. It is substituted for wafer-sealing self-mailers, keeping foldouts and gatefolds from coming apart during binding operations, and for holding something together (e.g., an instruction sheet in a pharmaceutical box) so it can be inserted automatically rather than by hand.

Remoistenable glue is the kind found on the inside edges of mailing envelopes, and it is used exclusively for envelopes, other return mail pieces, and stamps.

Permanent glue is designed to keep two panels together indefinitely and to penetrate and tear paper fiber before releasing. Common applications range from forming presentation folders to making CD sleeves. It is also

58

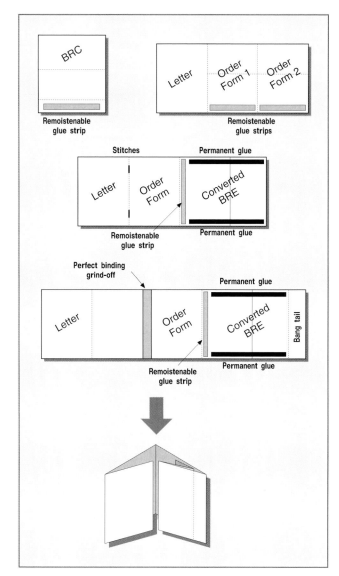

Common remoistenable glue applications.

used to hold folded pieces together during subsequent finishing operations like stitching. In this case, the glue is placed on extra material that will be trimmed off once the glue has served its purpose.

Gluing takes planning. Just as with other binding and finishing operations, the use of glue requires planning as far back as the design stage of print production.

Fugitive glue, for example, works best on penetration-resistant, highly calendered paper with heavily inked and coated surfaces. Matte, lightly coated enamel stock, offset paper, and sheets with heavy clay fillers can tear instead of releasing easily when the stock and glue are separated.

Permanent glues, on the other hand, are best when stock or paper adheres directly to stock or raw paper. Any "coating" like heavy ink coverage, varnishes, UV coating, and press powders can compromise glue adhesion.

Inkjet Addressing and Personalization

Some binderies specialize in traditional binding and finishing services, but others have also taken on mailing and distribution services. Inkjet addressing is one of those crossover services that can be considered a finishing activity, a mailing activity, or both.

Inkjet printing devices range in size from small to very large (called wide-format printers), and they are made for the consumer market and for business and printing needs. Inkjet printing is a nonimpact process. It uses tiny droplets of highly fluid ink that are given an electric charge and are sprayed toward the substrate either in a continuous fashion or in bursts of ink. Addresses and personalized information or messages are controlled by software programs.

One increasingly popular use for inkjet personalization is inside/outside imaging done by a unit attached to a saddle stitcher. This printer uses program software and

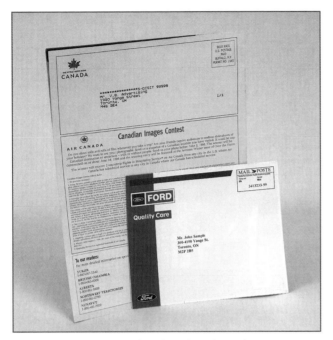

Example of products that have been laser-imaged or inkjet-printed.

database information to print names and addresses on the outside of publications—and also to place personalized messages on the inside or to even partly fill out tear-out business reply cards with personalized information.

Laminating

Laminating bonds two or more layers of material together with an adhesive. There are, however, two different reasons for and types of laminating in the bindery.

Mounting/laminating is done to provide stiffness or support to a product, for example, a point-of-purchase display. *Film laminating* is often used instead of coating. It provides a transparent decorative, protective layer for an ever-increasing amount of products, including menus,

cards, placemats, pocket calendars, outdoor posters, book covers, dust jackets, video slipcovers, cassettes, index tabs, maps, presentation folders, binders, brochures, case-bound books, and write-on/wipe-off wall posters. While both types of laminating can be done as part of bindery work, film laminating is by far the more prevalent bindery operation.

Film laminating bonds a thin, transparent film (polypropylene, polyester, acetate, or nylon) to the surface of a press sheet or other stock. The film is applied via the wet method or the thermal method. The *wet method* is more complicated and involves solvents or water, and the adhesive is applied to the film as the film is being applied to the substrate. The *thermal method*, which has become the dominant process in the last few years, uses heat (250–300°F) to bond the film, which has a pre-applied glue, to the stock.

Lamination is often combined with other specialty finishing processes. It can be done along with diecutting, scoring, embossing, and debossing. These processes, however, should be done after the film is applied. Laminating a product after embossing, for example, will smash the raised effect produced by embossing. As a rule, it is also best to do foil stamping before lamination to minimize adhesion problems.

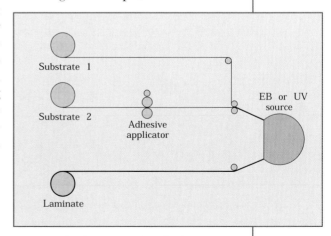

An example of a roll-to-roll laminating process.

Appendix A: Jobs in the Bindery

The work in a bindery ranges from basic manual labor to the operation of sophisticated electronically controlled machinery. Positions span entry-level work to supervisory roles.

Many bindery employees start as material handlers and, through on-the-job-training or apprenticeship, work their way up. Most bindery employees learn how to work with several different machines. Beginning machine helpers, for example, may be responsible for feeding the stitching, folding, and cutting equipment. They may also help package and move printed and finished materials into and out of the bindery. In a large operation, a folder operator may need to know how to set up and operate several types of folders, or he or she can advance to supervising all folding operations.

Checking employment ads and job descriptions for bindery workers shows that most employers want bindery workers who have the following qualifications:

- Strong basic math skills
- Mechanical aptitude
- Good hand-eye coordination and manual dexterity
- Skill in planning and measuring
- Ability to work with machinery that is increasingly automated and computer-controlled
- Ability to work well under pressure
- Patience and attention to detail
- High school degree

Being familiar with the other stages of print production and how they interact with binding and finishing process is always a plus.

Those who want to become bindery supervisors will need:

- Prior binding and finishing experience
- Thorough knowledge of the entire printing process
- Complete understanding of how print production processes affect and are affected by binding and finishing

61

- Strong math skills and mechanical aptitude
- Ability to communicate clearly with clients and technicians
- Leadership, management, and decision-making skills
- College degree (for some jobs)

Job Description Excerpts

The following excerpts provide insight into how the printing industry defines bindery work and what potential employers want bindery workers to be able to do in certain positions. The excerpts are meant for descriptive purposes only and are not to be considered as current legal job descriptions or as open job offerings. They provide good examples of the variety of skills bindery workers need, daily expectations in the workplace, and opportunities or pathways for growth and advancement.

Bindery Worker Senior

- Responsible for the operation of standard and complex bindery machines (right-angle folder, saddle-wire gatherer/stitcher, and programmable guillotine cutter), including setup, adjustment, and operation where multiple operations are performed on the printed material.
- Set up standard and complex mechanical folding, gathering, stitching, punching, and cutting machines.
- Operate all kinds of bindery equipment, including machines performing multiple operations.
- Keep all machines in good working order, making basic repairs as needed.
- Compile productivity data and preparing summary reports.
- Provide assistance to lower-level classifications in the setup and operation of machinery.

Bindery Worker

- Perform a variety of hand and machine operations to cut, trim, sort, assemble, fold, and bind printed materials.

- Review and clarify work order and specifications for due dates and processes to be used. Arrange work in processing and priority sequence. Plan and set up appropriate processing equipment.

- Advise other production unit staff on bindery equipment or processing requirements that affect planning and setups.

- Set up, operate, maintain, and repair bindery equipment such as hydraulic trimmers (including computer-controlled) and folding machines, some requiring critical planning and measurements.

- Set up perfect binders for single sheet, signature, or book production including glue selection, loading, temperature setting, and adjustment of pockets, grippers, and trimmers to job specifications.

- Operate large collators, gatherers, saddle stitchers in separate or ganged processing, including proper measurement and setup of parts and sections to paper size, weight, and characteristics.

- Work with drills, punches, perforators, staplers, padders (gluing operation), shrink wrappers, and strapping machines.

- May learn to operate, maintain, and repair stock moving equipment such as manual or powered pallet jacks, forklifts, and delivery truck.

- Test run all processing machine setups to be sure material is handled properly and meets order specifications.

- Monitor production equipment operation, making adjustments as required to maintain production and quality standards.

- Advise and guide trainees in setting up, operating, and adjusting equipment and in performing manual processing function.

- Repair and perform preventive and corrective maintenance to all equipment according to schedule or need. Replace worn blades, gears, bearings, springs, and motors on equipment as needed. Maintain production, maintenance and time records.

- Provide training, guidance, and work approval for trainees as required.
- Occasional contact with clients to clarify job specifications, to provide advice on bindery requirements, or resolve problems that may affect planning and layout of printed materials.

Cutter

- Adjust and operate all cutting equipment to prepare product to be collated or bound, ensuring the meeting of customer specifications.
- Review job tickets and plan work process to ensure meeting of customer specifications.
- Set up assigned machine to specifications, obtain approval of setup and run product.
- Monitor assigned machine during run to ensure adherence to specifications; unload machine and stack materials on carts; make adjustments as needed to maintain specifications and operating speed.
- Ensure the completion of jobs meeting quality and quantity requirements.
- Perform all required maintenance to machines according to departmental procedures.
- Troubleshoot machine problems, resolving if possible, notifying lead cutter or manager as needed.
- Complete special projects as assigned.
- Complete and maintain all required paperwork, records, documents, etc.
- Follow and comply with all safety and work rules and regulations. Maintain departmental housekeeping standards.

Finisher

- Obtain work assignments from supervisor.
- Pull all required materials to work on.
- Perform assigned activity to produce a completed product, to include setting up, drilling, stitching, grommeting, shrink wrapping, taping, cutting, marrying, collating, inserting, gluing, welding, etc., according to departmental procedures.
- Ensure accuracy of work being performed to produce the highest quality product at the lowest possible cost. Ensure production of the correct quantity.
- Obtain skids, load product onto skids according to procedures.
- Perform all tagging/labeling activities and move skid to shipping or staging area.
- Complete special projects as assigned.
- Complete and maintain all required paperwork, records, documents, etc.
- Follow and comply with all safety and work rules and regulations. Maintain departmental housekeeping standards.

Folding Utility

- Ensure orderly and timely flow of materials throughout folding.
- Supply cutters with paper; record count.
- Return flat paper to warehouse.
- Dump chip bins.
- Load and unload scrap trailer.
- Deliver empty baskets to machines.
- May cut paper when needed.
- Relieve operators when needed.
- Serve as backup to buffer manager.
- Supply machines with raw materials (fill gum bottles, empty trash, pull finished goods from machine and deliver to printing or shipping).
- Demonstrate good housekeeping.
- Work in a safe manner.

65

Job requirements and descriptions of duties in this section were compiled based on information found at the following websites: www.doer.state.mn.us/stfcs-ac/CSPCS-B/b-2402.htm, http://www.hr.das.state.or.us/hrsd/class/2412.HTM, and www.gain.net.

Bindery job descriptions can be found on the following sites:

- **www.gain.net** – the website for the Graphic Arts Technical Foundation and Printing Industries of America. Job descriptions are in a members-only area

- **teched.vt.edu/gcc/HTML/CareerInfo/GCBindery.html** – the website for Graphic Comm Central. Contains job descriptions from the U.S. Dictionary of Occupational Titles (DOT) plus job listings.

- **www.dictionary-occupationaltitles.net/** – the website for O°NET, the Occupational Information Network, developed by the U.S. Department of Labor. Comprehensive database and directory of occupational titles, worker competencies, job requirements, and resources; includes the *Dictionary of Occupational Titles,* the *Directory of Occupational Titles,* and the *Occupational Job Outlook.* For information about bindery work and workers from the *Occupational Job Outlook,* see Appendix B.

Appendix B: Occupational Outlook

The following occupational information was excerpted from the U.S. Bureau of Labor Statistics website in January 2003. For the complete version of this information, visit www.bls.gov/oco/ocos232.htm.

Occupational Outlook Handbook, 2002-03 Edition
U.S. Department of Labor / Bureau of Labor Statistics
Bookbinders and Bindery Workers

Nature of the Work

The process of combining printed sheets into finished products such as books, magazines, catalogs, folders, directories, or product packaging is known as "binding." Binding involves cutting, folding, gathering, gluing, stapling, stitching, trimming, sewing, wrapping, and other finishing operations. Bindery workers operate and maintain the machines that perform these various tasks.

Job duties depend on the kind of material being bound. In firms that do edition binding, for example, workers bind books produced in large numbers, or "runs." Job binding workers bind books produced in smaller quantities. In firms specializing in library binding, workers repair books and provide other specialized binding services to libraries. Pamphlet binding workers produce leaflets and folders, and manifold binding workers bind business forms such as ledgers and books of sales receipts. Blankbook binding workers bind blank pages to produce notebooks, checkbooks, address books, diaries, calendars, and note pads.

Some types of binding and finishing consist of only one step. Preparing leaflets or newspaper inserts, for example, require only folding. Binding of books and magazines, on the other hand, requires a number of steps.

Bookbinders and bindery workers assemble books and magazines from large, flat, printed sheets of paper. Skilled workers operate machines that first fold printed sheets into "signatures," which are groups of pages arranged sequentially. Bookbinders then sew, stitch, or glue the assembled signatures together, shape the book bodies with presses and trimming machines, and reinforce them with glued fabric strips. Covers are created separately, and glued, pasted, or stitched onto the book bodies. The books then undergo a variety of finishing operations, often including wrapping in paper jackets.

Bookbinders and bindery workers in small shops may perform many binding tasks, while those in large shops usually are assigned only one or a few operations, such as operating complicated manual or electronic guillotine paper cutters or folding machines. Others specialize in adjusting and preparing equipment, and may perform minor repairs as needed.

Employment

In 2000, bookbinders and bindery workers held about 115,000 jobs, including 9,600 working as skilled bookbinders and 105,000 working as bindery workers.

Although some large libraries and commercial book publishers have their own bindery operations, employing some bookbinders and bindery workers, the majority of jobs are in commercial printing plants. The largest employers of bindery workers are bindery trade shops—these companies specialize in providing binding services for printers without binderies or whose printing production exceeds their binding capabilities. Few publishers maintain their own manufacturing facilities, so most contract out the printing and assembly of books to commercial printing plants or bindery trade shops.

Training, Other Qualifications, and Advancement

Most bookbinders and bindery workers learn the craft through on-the-job training. Inexperienced workers usually are assigned simple tasks such as moving paper from cutting machines to folding machines. They learn basic binding skills, including the characteristics of paper and how to cut large sheets of paper into different sizes with the least amount of waste. As workers gain experience, they advance to more difficult tasks and learn to operate one or more pieces of equipment. Usually, it takes one to three months to learn to operate the simpler machines but it can take up to one year to become completely familiar with more complex equipment, such as computerized binding machines.

Excerpted from: Bureau of Labor Statistics, U.S. Department of Labor, *Occupational Outlook Handbook, 2002-03 Edition*, Bookbinders and Bindery Workers, on the Internet at http://www.bls.gov/oco/ocos232.htm.

Glossary

Accordion fold. Two or more folds parallel to each other with adjacent folds in opposite directions, resembling the bellows of an accordion. Alternative term: *fanfold*.

Adhesive binding. Applying a glue or another, usually hot-melt, substance along the backbone edges of assembled, printed sheets or folded signatures. The book or magazine cover is applied directly on top of the tacky adhesive. Alternative term: *perfect binding*.

Against the grain. Folding or cutting paper at right angles to the grain direction of the paper. Alternative term: *across the grain*.

Air table. A guillotine cutter bed equipped with tiny air holes that create a cushion of air between the paper pile and the table. This reduces friction, allowing the paper to be moved with greater ease.

Assembling. Collecting individual sheets or signatures in a complete set with pages in proper sequence and alignment. Assembling takes place prior to binding. Alternative terms: *collating; gathering; inserting*.

Back gauge. On a paper cutter, a movable metal stop that can be adjusted by the operator to the depth of the cut. Along with the side gauge, the back gauge also ensures that the paper pile is properly positioned under the knife so that the cuts will be square.

Back margin. The distance between the fold edge and the edge of the body of the type (text matter) next to the fold. Alternative terms: *binding margin; gutter margin*.

Backing. See *rounding and backing*.

Backlining. The piece of paper, muslin, or other material that reinforces the backs of books after rounding and backing.

Backup register. Correct relative position of the printing on one side of the sheet or web and the printing on the other side.

Basis weight. The weight in pounds of a ream (500 sheets) of paper cut to its basic size in inches. For example, 500 sheets of 25×38-in., 80-lb. coated paper will weigh eighty pounds. Alternative term: *substance weight*.

Batch counter. An auxiliary device for a saddle-stitcher that collects finished booklets into predetermined lots, freeing the operator from counting lots.

Bed. On a guillotine paper cutter, the flat metal surface on which the cutting is performed.

Belt delivery. On an adhesive binder, a method of conveying books from the nipping station to the in-line trimmer using a continuous belt.

Bind margin. The gutter or inner margin of a book, from the binding edge to the printed area.

Bind. To join the pages of a book together with thread, wire, adhesive, crash (a coarse fabric), or other methods, or enclose them in a cover.

Bindery. A facility or an area of a printing plant where binding and finishing operations (e.g., folding, joining signatures, and covering) are performed. Some trade binderies use the term "finishers," especially when they offer diverse binding and finishing services.

Binding. The process of joining together separate printed sheets or signatures to make books, magazines, catalogs, and booklets. Binding is also used as a general term to describe all finishing operations.

Binding dummy. Blank pages of the assembled signatures, stitched and trimmed to show the amount of compensation needed for creep.

Binding edge. The side of the publication where the signatures are joined together.

Binding marks. Trim marks, fold marks, and spine/collating marks added to a press sheet during imposition that serve as aids or guides for cutting, folding, and collating in the bindery.

Bleed. Pictures, lines, or solid colors that extend beyond the edge or edges of a page so that when margins are trimmed, the image is trimmed even with the edge of the page. Bleeds are usually at least 1/8 in., and some facilities use 1/4-in. bleeds.

Blow-in card feeder. An auxiliary feeder on saddle stitchers and adhesive binders that uses compressed air to add or "blow in" an insert, such as a reply card, that has been printed separately and will not be stitched into the publication.

Body. The printed text of a book not including the end papers or cover.

Book block. (1) The multiple signatures for a book assembled (stacked) into a single set in the proper sequence. Printers of magazines and other publications besides books may call this a "block" or a "lift." (2) In case binding, a book that has been folded, gathered, and stitched but not cased-in.

Buckle folder. A bindery machine in which two rollers push the printed sheet between two metal plates, stopping it and causing it to buckle at the entrance to the folder. A third roller working with one of the original rollers uses the buckle to fold the paper. Buckle folders are best suited for parallel folding.

Buckle plates. Two smooth, flat metal sheets that receive the paper that has come through the buckling mechanism on buckle or combination folders during binding and finishing. Alternative term: *fold plates.*

Building-in. Placing cased-in books in a forming and pressing machine that holds them tightly under heat and pressure while the adhesive is drying.

Bundling unit, automatic. An auxiliary device that tightly compresses stacks of signatures into more compact loads (logs) as they come off the delivery. The log protects the signatures from damage during handling and also has the benefit of tightening the folds.

Caliper. (1) A device that measures thickness. (2) The thickness of a sheet of paper or other material measured under specific conditions. Caliper is usually expressed in mils (thousandths of an inch). Paper thickness is measured with an instrument called a caliper gauge or micrometer.

Case. In book binding, the hardcovers into which bound signatures are affixed.

Case binding. The process that produces a hardcover book. Printed covering material is glued to rigid board material forming a hardcover "case," and the case is then affixed to the book with endpapers.

Casebound. A book bound with a stiff, hard cover.

Casing-in. Applying adhesive and combining a sewn and trimmed text with a cover (case).

Center marks. Positioning marks placed on the press sheet during imposition to help the press operator make sure that the press layout is centered on the printed sheet.

Clamp. (1) On an adhesive binder, a device that grips the book block firmly on either side and guides it into the milling station. (2) On a paper cutter, a movable metal bar that sits above and runs parallel to the paper pile.

Closed head. The uncut top of a signature.

Collate. The process of sorting the pages of a publication in the proper order.

Collating. A variant of gathering where cut, trimmed, or folded signatures or sheets are stacked one on top of another to form multiple layers. This form of gathering is used for adhesive binding, which requires collated signatures so that the glue can penetrate and bind each sheet together.

Collating marks. A distinctive numbered or other symbol printed on the folded edge or spine of signatures to denote the correct gathering sequence. The position of the mark is staggered from one signature to the next to show a pattern, allowing the bindery operator to visually check the order of the signatures. Alternative terms: *plugs; spine/collating marks.*

Comb binding. A curved or rake-shaped plastic strip inserted through slots punched along the binding edge of the sheet. See also: *mechanical binding.*

Combination folder. (1) The in-line finishing component of a publication or book web offset press that uses at least three different folds, such as the jaw, former, and chopper folds, to cut and fold the printed web into signatures that are shipped to a bindery. (2) A binding machine that has both knife and buckle folding mechanisms. Alternative term: *combi folder.*

Compensating stacker/counter. An automatic delivery device that alternates the layering of a stack of printed products by turning them 180° to offset the uneven thickness between face and spine of a book.

Computer-to-plate (CTP). A technology in which imaging systems receive fully paginated/imposed material electronically from computers and expose this information to plates in platesetters or imagesetters, without creating film intermediates. The output device uses lasers to write the printing dots directly to the plates from the information in the imposed digital files.

Conditioning. The complete and equal exposure of all areas of paper to accurately controlled and specified atmospheric conditions so that its moisture content throughout reaches equilibrium with the surrounding atmosphere. Temperature conditioning refers to bringing the paper's temperature into equilibrium with the atmosphere without removing its wrapping and exposing it to the atmosphere.

Continuous feeder. On a folder, a type of feeder that allows the operator to feed paper on a continual basis without stopping the folder. The continuous feeder is a long table upon which the operator stacks a pile of fanned, staggered sheets. Conveyor tapes on the pile feed table inch the pile forward to a stop mechanism, where sheets are drawn one at a time onto the infeed/lattice table.

Converting. Any manufacturing or finishing operation completed after printing in order to form the printed item into the final product. Bagmaking, coating, waxing, laminating, folding, slitting, gluing, box manufacture, and diecutting are some examples. Converting units may be attached to the end of the press, or the operation may be handled by a special outside facility.

Conveyor chain. (1) On a saddle stitcher, a continuous-loop moving chain with a number of saddle sections that moves under the feeder stations, receiving the folded signatures dropped from the feeder stations in sequence until a complete booklet (signature set) is formed. (2) On an adhesive binder, a continuous-loop chain that includes long "fingers" attached at intervals. These fingers push the signature off of the feeder tray and onto the raceway where it is guided to the next feeder tray. Alternative term: *gathering chain.*

Conveyor tapes. Narrow continuous moving belts that transport booklets between sections of a machine.

Counter die. On a folder, a die with recessed surface (groove) or a gap between the two halves that is used with a wheel-like scoring die (which has a raised score blade) to score the paper before it is folded.

Cover feeder. (1) On a saddle-stitcher, a special feeding station that scores, folds, and delivers heavier cover papers onto the saddle. (2) On an adhesive binder, a device that feeds one cover at a time. The cover feeder includes scoring die rollers, which score the cover where folds will be placed. Types of cover feeders include vertical pile feeders, horizontal pile feeders, and stream feeder.

Cover nipper. The area in a perfect binder's cover feeder in which each cover is folded and then pushed around the spine.

Cover papers. A heavy paper designed to serve as the outer layer and protective cover of a booklet, such as an annual report or journal, or other paper application, such as posters, postcards, and greeting cards. Cover papers are similar to offset papers, except that they are thicker.

Covering. The process of pasting endpapers to a hardback book and drying them under pressure. See also: *casing-in; building-in.*

Crash. A coarse fabric used to strengthen the joints of casebound books. It is placed over the binding edge of a book before it is cased-in to help hold the book within its cover.

Creep. With saddle-stitched publications, the slight but cumulative outward thrust of the edges of each inserted spread or signature beyond the edges of the signature that encloses it. This results in a progressively smaller trim size on the inside pages. Creep is counteracted during the imposition phase by moving the page a tiny bit inward. Alternative terms: *binder's creep; push-out; shingling, thrust.*

Cross-direction. The position across the grain, or at a right angle to the machine direction, on a sheet of paper. The stock is not as strong and is more susceptible to relative humidity in the cross-direction.

Cross-grain. Folding at right angles to the binding edge of a book, or at a right angle to the direction of the grain in the paper stock. Folding the stock against the grain.

Crossover. A photo, headline, or other image that extends across the gutter between the left-hand and right-hand pages of a two-page spread in a magazine, book, or other multipage product. Alternative terms: *breakacross.*

Curl. The bending or arcing of paper as the result of structural differences between the two sides of paper, usually due to differences in temperature or moisture content.

Cutline indicator. On a paper cutter, a device that shines a thin line of light on the positioned paper pile, showing exactly where the cut will be made.

Cutting. The operations performed to cut apart sheets of stock or printed materials. In the bindery, cutting is almost always done using a single-knife guillotine cutter.

Cutting angle. On a paper cutter, the beveled shape to which the cutting edge of the knife is sharpened. The angle of the bevel varies depending on the material being cut.

Cutting stick. A long square rod, generally made of a tough plastic, that is inserted into a groove on the cutting table immediately beneath the cutting knife and that functions as a counter cutting tool. When the knife slices through a pile of stock, it touches the cutting stick instead of the cutting table, which prevents the knife from breaking or becoming dull too quickly.

Cutting table. The bed of the cutter that supports the lift of stock that will be cut. Newer models are equipped with an air table that allows the paper to be moved with greater ease.

Deflector plate. A special sheet detector that is inserted to bypass any buckle plates not needed for a particular folding job.

Delivery. The section of a folder, saddle stitcher, or adhesive binder where the folded paper, stitched and trimmed booklet, or trimmed-adhesive bound book exits the machine for stacking or packaging.

Density. The weight of paper relative to its volume. Dense papers are more compact with their fibers more tightly bonded together. In softer, bulkier, more porous papers, fiber clusters can swell or shrink without much change in the overall dimensions of the sheet.

Die. A pattern of sharp knives or metal tools used to stamp, cut, or emboss specific shapes, designs, and letters into a substrate.

Die, embossing. A heated or cold brass or steel tool that impresses a raised design into a paper substrate. Unlike a cutting die, the edge of an embossing die is not sharp.

Die stamping. Using a brass or other hard metal die to stamp a book case with ink or metallic foil.

Diecut. A printed subject cut to a specific shape with sharp steel rules on a press.

Diecutting. Using sharp steel rules to slice paper or board to a specific shape on a platen press or specialized stamping press. Diecuts are common in labels, greeting cards, and pop-up books. Diecuts are also made to form the shape of packages before they are folded and glued.

Digital design file. The end result of the design stage, a computer file that contains all the pages and their elements (e.g., text in the chosen font) in a form meant to be printed. Photographic images, illustrations, and logos are submitted as separate files that are linked to the main file.

Digital printing. An umbrella term for a number of non-impact electronic printing processes. Two of the most prominent are inkjet printing and electrostatic (electrophotography). Inkjet involves spraying ink through nozzles onto the surface of the substrate. Electrostatic printing involves the use of a laser to "write" an image on a drum. The image is then coated with toner, a kind of powder ink, which is then transferred to the substrate by heat and pressure.

Dimensional stability. The degree to which paper maintains its size in the face of temperature and moisture content changes, as well as applied stresses.

Direct-imaging press. A press in which the printing plates are imaged directly on the press rather than away from the press, as when a separate platesetter is used in a computer-to-plate (CTP) workflow.

Dog-ears. Bent-over corners of paper that can occur when paper is fed through the press, as the corner catches and folds over. Dog-eared sheets can keep the paper from feeding smoothly through finishing and binding equipment. Folding equipment infeed systems can also create dog-ears.

Double-sixteen. A folder that takes a thirty-two-page form and folds it as two separate or inserted sixteen-page forms.

Double-thirty-two. A folder that takes a sixty-four-page form and folds it as two separate or inserted thirty-two-page forms.

Dummy. (1) A preliminary layout showing the position of illustrations, text, folds, and other design elements as they are to appear in the printed piece. (2) A set of blank pages prepared to show the size, shape, style, and general appearance of a book, pamphlet, or other printed piece.

Edge trimming. On a folder, the process of using slitters riding on the edges of the sheet to cut off the portion of the press sheet containing the press marks.

Edition binding. See *case binding*.

Embossing. A finishing operation that involves sandwiching the paper between a relief pattern die and a recessed counter die under heat and pressure. The result is a permanent raised pattern in the paper.

Emulsion glue. A cold-applied glue based on water-soluble polyvinyl acetate (PVA) products and used in adhesive binding.

End leaf. A strong paper used to combine and secure the body of a book to its case. One leaf is pasted against the book's front cover and one against the back cover. Alternative terms: *end papers; end sheets.*

End product. The final package or printed piece ready for customer use after all folding, gluing, and other binding, finishing, and/or converting operations are completed.

Ergonomics. The process of making the workplace safer for workers by designing work methods and equipment to reduce injuries.

Face. The side of the page opposite the spine. When a multipage product is closed, the spine is on the left and the face is on the right.

Feed table. The section of a cover feeder for an adhesive binder that contains adjustable side and back stops to support the pile of covers and accommodate different size covers.

Feeder station. On a saddle stitcher or adhesive binder, the section of the feeder that holds the folded signatures in piles, removes signatures one at a time, and drops them onto the conveyor chain. Alternative terms: *gatherer; hopper; magazine; pocket; signature feeding station.*

Feeder unit. The section of an an adhesive binder that has a separate feeding station for each signature. The number of feeding stations may vary from ten or fewer to more than thirty-two, depending on how many signatures make up the finished product.

Film laminating. A finishing process in which a plastic film is bonded by heat and pressure to a printed sheet to provide protection or enhance appearance.

Finishing. All forms of completing graphic arts production, including folding, trimming, and assembling sections; binding by sewing, wire stitching, or gluing; and die-cutting or gold stamping. Finishing can also refer to converting processes that change printed stock into another form, e.g., bags and boxes.

Flexography. A method of rotary letterpress printing characterized by the use of flexible, rubber or plastic plates with raised image areas and fluid, rapid-drying inks. This process employs a relief principle, meaning that the image area is raised above the surface of the printing plate. Ink is transferred to the relief areas and then transferred to the substrate under pressure. The plates are made of a flexible polymer material, which is why it is called "flex"-ography.

Fold. Bending and creasing a sheet of paper as required to form a printed product.

Fold marks. Guides on the original copy and printed sheet that indicate where a printed piece will be folded and that aid in setting up the folder. Fold marks are usually indicated with a dotted or broken line.

Fold plates. See *buckle plates*.

Folded to paper. Sheets folded without regard to alignment of headers, footers, and other images throughout the signatures. Press sheets with printing on only one side of the form are folded to paper because backup register is not a consideration.

Folded to print. Sheets folded so that the headers, footers, and other image areas from page to page are aligned from one signature to another.

Folder. The machine that bends and creases printed sheets of paper to particular specifications during binding and finishing. The process itself is called folding.

Folder, quad. A machine that folds and delivers four sixteen-page signatures separately or as two thirty-two-page signatures from a single press sheet with sixty-four pages printed across it.

Folding. The process of bending and creasing paper to form a finished piece or a multipage document. Folding is usually done mechanically by machines that are increasingly computer-controlled. Hand folding is also done, but binderies try to avoid this labor-intensive, expensive process.

Folding dummy. A mockup that shows the placement of page heads, the binding edge, and the gripper and side guide edges, as well as the page sequence and the arrangement of signatures. It is made from a blank press-size sheet of the job stock that is folded and marked with such information as page numbers and Xs to indicate the gripper (lead) edge and side-guide edge when the work is printed on a sheetfed press. It can also be used to determine which sides of each page need single-trim and double-trim allowances. Inserting and collating can also be illustrated.

Folding unit. The section on a folder that contains the components required to make the fold. The other two main sections of a folder are the infeed and the delivery.

Foot. The bottom of a page.

Foot margin. The distance between the bottom edge of the body of type (text matter) on a page and the bottom edge of the trimmed page. Alternative term: *tail margin.*

Footer. A book's title or chapter title printed at the bottom of a page. A drop folio (page number) may or may not be included. Alternative term: *running foot.*

Form. Either side of a signature. A form usually contains a multiple of eight pages, but may be more or less.

Forwarding. Backing, rounding, shaping, lining up, and head banding, among other operations performed before a casebound book is covered.

Full bleed. An image extending to all four edges of the trimmed sheet leaving no visible margins.

Gathering. Assembling multiple signatures into a single set in the proper sequence, sometimes called a "book block."

Glue pot. The container that holds the glue on an adhesive binder.

Gluing unit. On an adhesive binder, a hot-melt glue applicator comprised of a glue pot and applicator rollers that applies glue to the spine and/or the sides of the book.

Gluing-off. Applying glue to the spine of a book that is to be casebound.

Grain direction. In papermaking, the alignment of the fibers in the direction of web travel. On all roll papers, grain direction is lengthwise on the web, parallel to the direction of web travel.

Grain-long paper. With a rectangular sheet, paper in which the grain runs along the longer dimension.

Grain-short paper. With a rectangular sheet, paper in which the grain runs along the shorter dimension.

Graphic arts workflow. The sequence of steps involved in producing a printed piece. Production workflow may vary slightly from one plant to another, but the stages of production are basically the same throughout the industry.

Gravure. An intaglio printing process in which minute depressions, sometimes called cells, that form the image area are engraved or etched below the nonimage area in the surface of the printing cylinder. The cylinder is immersed in a fluid ink, and the excess ink is scraped off by a blade, leaving the ink in the etched areas beneath the surface. When paper or another substrate comes in contact with the printing cylinder, the ink is drawn out of the etched areas and transferred to the substrate.

Grind-off. In adhesive binding, a step preparatory to gluing in which the spine of the folded signatures are roughened to allow the glue to penetrate and bind the pages.

Gripper edge. The leading edge of the paper that rests at the head stops and is grabbed by mechanical fingers known as grippers. The press operator typically marks the gripper edge with an "XXX" before sending the job to the binding and finishing area.

Grippers. (1) The metal clamps or metal fingers that grasp and hold a registered sheet in position as it travels through a sheetfed press. (2) On rotary-drum feed systems for an adhesive binder, the cam-mounted metal fingers that grab a signature, pull it down around the gripper drum, and deposit it on the feeder tray or conveyor chain.

Guillotine cutter. A device with a long, heavy sloping blade that descends to a table or bed and slices through a stack of paper. Guillotine cutters come in a variety of models and size, but they all share the following common components: a knife, cutting stick, cutting table, side and back gauges, and a clamp.

Gutter. (1) A gutter is a standard size gap that separates a design or text area into columns. (2) The inside margin between facing pages, or the margin at the binding edge. Alternative terms: *gutter margin; back margin.*

Hard materials. From the perspective of the paper cutter operator, one of two broad classifications of difficult-to-cut substrates based on the general hardness or softness of materials. Hard materials include art board, gummed papers, cardboard, and plastic foils.

Hazard Communication Standard. Often referred to as "Haz-Com," a program required by OSHA that communicates chemical hazards, including the following provisions that directly affect binding and finishing production areas: (1) maintain a chemical inventory, or record, of every chemical used in the plant, (2) secure a material safety data sheet (MSDS) for every chemical used in the plant and make these readily available to all workers, (3) label containers in a prescribed manner to allow production workers to quickly assess any hazards associated with the chemical, (4) provide proper personal protective equipment (PPE) to protect the workers from hazards such as excessive noise or chemical splashes, and (5) provide employee training on how to recognize chemical hazards and protect themselves.

Head. The top of a page, book, or printing form.

Head margin. The distance between the top edge of the trimmed page and the top edge of the body of type (text matter) on a page.

Head stop. A stationary device on the folder's register board that stops the forward movement of a sheet so that each sheet is positioned in exactly the same spot.

Head trim. The amount of paper that is cut off above the head margin; usually about 1/8 in. (3 mm).

Headband. An ornamental strip of reinforced cotton or silk attached to the top and bottom of the inner back of a bound book.

Header. A book's title or a chapter title printed at the top of a page and often with a folio (page number). Alternative term: *running head.*

High-resolution scanning. Using an electronic scanner to capture a photographic image digitally at resolutions equal to or greater than 300 dots per inch (dpi) and store the information in a computer file.

Hopper. A device with side and rear guides that holds a stack of the signatures in place in the feed unit of an adhesive binder or saddle stitcher.

Hot foil stamping. Using a heated flat steel die and colored foil or gold leaf to press a design into a book cover, a sheet of paper, or another substrate. The foil fuses to the paper to create a metallic image in the shape of the die. The die may be used alone (in blind stamping) if no color or other ornamentation is necessary.

Hot-melt glues. Any of several glues in adhesive binding that are applied at temperatures between 350 and 400°F (177–204°C), with some having application temperatures as low as 250°. Ethyl vinyl acetate copolymers (EVAs), the most common hot-melt glue used in the printing industry, are composed of about 50% polymer mixed with 30% resin (for adhesion) and 15% wax softeners (for added flexibility).

Humidity, relative. The amount of moisture present in the air, expressed as a percentage of the amount of moisture required to saturate the air at a given temperature.

Hydraulic lifts. A hydraulically operated device that raises a load to the height desired by the worker.

Imagesetter. A high-resolution device used to output fully paginated text and graphic images onto photographic film, paper, or plate.

Imposition. Arranging the pages of a job on a printing form during the prepress stage of production so that when printed, folded, trimmed, and bound, all content appears in the proper sequence and orientation. Control marks needed by the press, finishing, and binding operators are also placed on the imposition. Page layout is the process of defining where repeating elements such as headlines, text, and folios (page numbers) will appear on multiple pages throughout a document, while imposition can be thought of as defining where these completed pages will appear on much larger sheets of paper. The binding method affects the imposition and assembly order. Imposition involves not only pages but other print job graphics as well, such as multiple copies of a label. Imposition in a digital print workflow is done using special imposition software. Alternative term: *press sheet layout.*

Imposition layout. A guide that indicates folding sequence, number of pages and signatures used, guide and gripper edges, and cutting and scoring lines for a specific job.

Infeed. Part of a folder composed of a table, where paper is stacked and system components guide sheets into the folding unit. The term is also used to identify where stock enters presses and other types of printing and binding equipment.

Infrared dryer. A unit in which an assembly of lamps emitting infrared radiation that generate heat to evaporate water from the PVA adhesives used in adhesive binding.

Inkjet addressing unit. An auxiliary device that uses inkjet technology to address publications and/or print personalized messages in-line with saddle stitchers and adhesive binders. The inkjet units are interfaced with a central database of addresses and other information.

Inkjet printing. A nonimpact printing process in which a stream of electrostatically charged microscopic ink droplets are projected onto a substrate at a high velocity from a pressurized system.

In-line finishing. Manufacturing operations such as numbering, addressing, sorting, folding, diecutting, and converting that are performed as part of a continuous operation right after the printing section on a press or on a single piece of equipment as part of the binding process.

In-line trimming. (1) On an adhesive binder, trimming books on the head, face, and foot using a three-knife trimmer. (2) On a saddle stitcher, trimming books on the head, face, and foot using a three-knife trimmer.

Insert. (1) A page that is printed separately and then bound into the main publication. (2) An advertising leaflet often on low-grade paper that is placed inside a periodical or newspaper.

Inserting. A variant of gathering or collating that involves assembling signatures one inside another in sequence. This form of gathering is used for saddle stitching.

Job jacket. The work order, or control form, on which the instructions for each phase of production are written. The job jacket may also contain the original copy, photos, and line art for the job. The following information is typically found on a job jacket: (a) paper used for the job, (b) ink colors used for the job, (c) quantity required by the customer, (d) types of proofs created, (e) type of finishing operations required, (f) type of binding operations required, (g) grain direction and size of the job, and (h) how the job will be packaged. Also known as *job ticket*.

Jog. (1) Moving the components of a machine in small increments. (2) To align flat, stacked sheets or signatures to a common edge, either manually or with a vibrating table or hopper. Some in-line finishing systems are equipped with a jogger-stacker that piles and aligns folded signatures as they are delivered.

Jogger. A mechanical table used to square a pile of paper so that cuts will be even throughout the pile. The jogger has at least two sidewalls at 90° angles to the table surface. The jogger can be tilted so the paper pile sits against the sidewalls with the aid of gravity. When a motor is turned on, the paper pile is vibrated, squaring it against the sidewalls.

Joint. The flexible portion of a casebound book where the cover meets the spine. It functions as a hinge, permitting the cover to be opened and closed without damage to the spine. Alternative term: *hinge*.

Knife. (1) A sharp steel blade that trims excess from sheets and/or cuts them to a specific size. (2) The blade used in conjunction with folding rollers on a knife folder.

Knife folder. A type of folder in which three or four blades at different levels and at right angles to each other force the paper between the folding rollers. The sheet of paper is pushed from one knife folding mechanism to the next until the desired number of folds has been made.

Laminating. The process of using heat and pressure to apply a clear material to one or both sides of a printed piece to provide a high-gloss appearance and durability. Restaurant menus and posters are products that are often laminated.

Lap. The overhang or extra edge, created by folding the signature off center, that is required for feeding mechanisms to grab and pull open the signature to the center spread when being inserted. A typical lap value is 3/8 in. Alternative term: *lip*.

Lay. The arrangement and position of printed forms on a press sheet.

Leaf. (1) A separate, usually blank, sheet of paper in a book. (2) Pigmented stamping material used to decorate book edges.

Leg. One of two appendages of a wire stitch that is bent down to secure the signatures of a saddle-stitched product.

Letterpress scoring. The use of a letterpress platen press for scoring. The presses use either a male die and matrix set or a scoring/creasing rule and channel-creasing matrix to raise a ridge on the inside of the fold.

Library binding. A book bound in conformance with the specifications of the American Library Association. The requirements include stitched signatures, sewn-on four-cord thread, strong end papers, muslin-reinforced end papers, and flannel backlining extended into the boards.

Lift table. A mechanically operated device that raises a load to the height desired by the worker. Lift tables often sit next to the cutter table and use sensors that automatically raise the table to the necessary height.

Lining. The reinforcing material pasted on the spine of a casebound book before the cover is applied.

Lip. See *lap.*

Litho scoring. A method of scoring performed in-line on a lithographic printing press using a flexible scoring rule on the impression cylinder.

Lithography. A printing process in which the image carrier is chemically treated so that the nonimage areas are receptive to water (i.e., dampening or fountain solution) and repel ink while the image areas are receptive to ink and repel water.

Lockout/tagout. A standard from OSHA that addresses the safety precautions for servicing and maintaining machinery, where unexpected start-up of machinery could injure employees. Lockout describes the use of locks on energy sources to avoid accidental activation of equipment. Tagout describes the conditions when a lock cannot be used. Here, tags or labels with lockout procedures are used in place of physical lockout.

Log. Signatures tightly compressed in a stack through the use of bundling equipment.

Loose-leaf binding. A binding method which uses rings that can open and close and upon which individual sheets can be inserted and removed at will. Alternative term: *mechanical binding.*

Machine guards. Barriers to protect workers from the moving parts and pinch points on industrial equipment such as gears, chains, and rollers. Machine guards also cover electrical hazards and heated elements that could cause burns.

Makeready. All the operations necessary to get the press ready to print the current job. Makeready includes mounting the plates on the press, loading paper, filling the ink fountains, and making sure the press is printing the correct color and register for the job.

Margin. Standard areas surrounding the image part of a page that extend from the edge of the page to the image area.

Material safety data sheet (MSDS). A product specification form used to record information about the hazardous chemicals and other health and physical hazards connected with a product, along with guidelines covering exposure limits and other precautions. Employers are required to compile and maintain files of this information under the OSHA Hazard Communication Standard set forth by the U.S. federal government and make this information readily available to all workers.

Materials handling and storage. The various operations involved in moving material and product through a printing plant, including warehousing and shipping.

Mechanical binding. Clasping individual sheets together with plastic, small wire, or metal rings. Two examples are three-ring binding and spiral binding.

Milling head. The device on an adhesive binder that grinds off the folded spines of the signatures to expose the individual sheets to the glue.

Misregister. Printed images that are incorrectly positioned, either in reference to each other, to the sheet's edges, or from one side of the sheet to the other.

79

Multiple-up imposition. A layout with two or more duplicates of the same image or several images on a press sheet. Alternative term: *step-and-repeat layout*.

Nip. A crease line at the joint of a case-bound book. It gives the book uniform bulk and reduces the swelling caused by the sewing thread. See also: *smash*.

Nipping. In binding, squeezing and clamping books or signatures after sewing or stitching to remove excess air and reduce the swell caused by stitching. Hard papers are nipped, and soft pages are smashed. See also: *smash*.

Notch binding. Small serrations cut in the spine of a perfect-bound book and filled with glue. This method eliminates the need to mill material off the spine of the book.

Offline. Used to describe standalone machines or operations.

One-up. Printing a single image once on a press sheet.

OSHA. An acronym for the Occupational Safety and Health Administration, the body of the federal government that helps ensure safe work standards.

Overcut. In paper cutting, the condition in which the paper at the top of the pile is cut shorter than paper further down.

Page layout. The process of positioning text, pictures, and other image elements on a page using a desktop publishing program, such as QuarkXPress, Adobe InDesign, or Adobe PageMaker.

Pallet. A low, sturdy platform on which materials may be placed for handling in quantity.

Parallel fold. Any fold made in a sheet of paper or other substrate that is oriented in a direction parallel to a previous fold. A single fold can be called a parallel fold because it creates two panels that are parallel to each other.

Parallel to the grain. In the same direction as the grain of the paper. Alternative terms: *along the grain; with the grain*.

Perfect binding. See *adhesive binding*.

Perforating. The process of mechanically slotting or punching a row of small holes or incisions into or through a sheet of paper to permit part of it to be detached, to guide in folding, to allow air to escape from signatures, or to prevent wrinkling and the occurrence of dog-ears when folding. A perforation may be indicated by a series of printed lines, or it may be blind; in other words, without a printed indication on the cutline. Alternative term: *perf*.

Pinch point. A area where two rollers or cylinders first contact each other, with the potential of grabbing an operator's hand or hair. Gears, chains, and rollers are examples of pinch point areas. Machine guards are used to protect workers from pinch points and moving parts on industrial equipment.

Plastic binding. A form of mechanical binding using plastic strips, combs, or coils in place of stitching. The binding edge is punched with slots or holes through which the formed plastic material is inserted.

Plate. A thin metal, plastic, or paper sheet that serves as the image carrier in many printing processes.

Platemaking. In conventional printing, preparing a printing plate from a film or flat, exposing it through the flat, and developing or processing and finishing it so that is ready to be used on press. In computer-to-plate (CTP) operations in which imaging systems receive fully paginated/imposed material electronically from computers and expose this information directly to plates in platesetters or imagesetters, without creating film intermediates.

Pocket. See *feeder station*.

Points. A method of describing the thickness of paper; one point equals one thousandth of an inch. For example, a sheet of 0.004-in. stock is 4 points thick.

Polyurethane adhesives (PUR). A type of hot-melt glue used in adhesive binding that is applied at temperatures between 250–300°F. At room temperature, PUR is in solid form, and it is melted in air-tight premelters.

Polyvinyl acetate (PVA). A water-soluble glue used in adhesive binding and applied cold. Similar to regular craft glue, it has a long natural drying time of 8–12 hours that can be reduced to 3–4 minutes by using gas, infrared, or high-frequency drying.

Post binder. A loose-leaf binding method in which straight rods instead of rings are used to hold the pages together. The binder can be expanded as the bulk of the contents increases.

Postpress. In a graphic arts workflow, the activities that take place after presswork, specifically binding and finishing, but also including shipping, mailing, and distribution.

Preflighting. (1) In prepress, an orderly preventive procedure using a printed checklist or special software to verify that all components of a job (e.g., digital text files and high-resolution image files) are present and correct prior to submitting the document for high-resolution output and to identify potential problems that could cause rework or even rerunning a whole job. (2) In the bindery, the orderly preventive procedure using a printed checklist to ascertain the completeness of a newly arrived job.

Premelter. A separate piece of equipment attached to the gluing station of an adhesive binder and used to gradually and uniformly melt the glue.

Prepress. The stage of graphic arts workflow that readies the job elements to be printed. It can be described as what happens from the time a digital file has been completely designed until it is actually printed. It includes,

among other operations, preflighting, proofing, and platemaking. Alternative term: *premedia*.

Press. The stage of graphic arts workflow that involves putting ink on paper or other substrate. It includes all the tasks needed to get the press ready to print, the print run (pressrun) itself, and press washup afterward. Alternative term: *presswork*.

Press sheet layout. See *imposition*.

Pressrun. The phase of presswork that commences once the press sheet matches the proof. It involves operations that affect binding and finishing, such as maintaining registration, printing the correct number of sheets, monitoring quality control variables that affect the useable number of sheets, and handling materials carefully so that they feed properly into folding machines and other equipment.

Printer's spread. A pair of pages in a certain order so that printing, folding, and binding yield the sequence in which the reader or recipient needs to see them.

Process control. Identifying, measuring, and controlling measurable variables in the printing and binding process in order to produce a high-quality product. Examples of variables include ink density, image registration, product trim size, and glue thickness on binding. Once a variable is measured, production personnel can track and benchmark quality numerically.

Proofs. A simulation of the printed product that provides the chance to verify that color, placement, and other factors meet expectations.

Push-out. See *creep*.

Reader's spread. A pair of pages positioned across the binding edge, or gutter, from each other so they can be read or understood in the correct order after the book is bound; e.g., pages 6 and 7 of a book.

Ream. Five-hundred (500) sheets of paper.

Register. Overall agreement in the position of printing detail on a press sheet, especially the alignment of two or more overprinted colors in multicolor presswork. Register may be observed by agreement of overprinted register marks on a press sheet. Also refers to the correct placement of printed material on both sides of a press sheet. Alternative term: *registration.*

Register marks. Small reference patterns, guides, or crosses placed on press sheets to aid in aligning overprinted colors on press sheets.

Rework. Redoing an entire job or a portion of the job due to a mistake made in any stage of production.

Right-angle fold. Any fold made in a sheet of paper or other substrate that is oriented at a 90° angle to a previous fold.

Rotary scoring. Usually done on a folder, a method of scoring that uses circular scoring dies mounted on a shaft and a counter die.

Roughening head. The cutting head on an adhesive binder that prepares the backbone fibers for exposure to the glue.

Rounding and backing. Shaping a book to fit its cover. Rounding gives books a convex spine and a concave fore-edge. Backing makes the spine wider than the thickness of the rest of the book to provide a shoulder against which the cardboard front and back covers rest. It also provides the hinge crease for the joints of the book. See also: *nip; smash.*

Saddle. On a saddle stitcher, the bar on which the opened signatures are draped as they move through the machine.

Saddle stitching. Binding multiple sheets by opening the signatures in the center and gathering and stitching them with a wire through the fold line. The folded sheets rest on supports called saddles as they are transported through the stitcher. Booklets, brochures, and pamphlets are most often bound this way. Alternative terms: *saddle wire; wire stitch.*

Saddle stitcher. A machine that performs saddle stitching. Stitchers range from small manually powered models to large automated machines. Alternative terms: *saddle binder; stitcher; wire stitcher.*

Scoring. Making a crease in paper by impressing a steel rule against the paper surface. This ruptures the paper fibers, creating a line for making crisp, accurate folds on heavier stocks like text and cover sheets.

Screen printing. A printing process in which a squeegee forces ink through a porous mesh, synthetic, or silk image carrier, or screen, covered by a stencil that blocks the nonimage areas. The ink pressed through the open image areas of the screen forms the image on the substrate.

Sewing. In bookbinding, fastening printed signatures together with needle and thread or cord.

Sheet curl. A paper problem that results in a pile of sheets that does not lay flat but curves in one direction. This can cause infeed problems with finishing and binding equipment. Sheet curl can happen when paper absorbs too much moisture on one side of the sheet during printing.

Sheeter. A machine that cuts roll paper into sheets. Sheeters are used as an alternative delivery on a web press (instead of a folder) or as a feeding system on a sheetfed press, in which case roll paper is cut into sheets that are then fed individually into the press.

Sheetfed press. A printing press that feeds and prints on individual sheets of paper (or another substrate).

Sheeting. The process of cutting rolls of paper into sheets to be printed.

Shingling. See *creep.*

Shrink wrap. Using heat to affix a thin plastic material around printed and bound products to prepare them for shipment.

Side gauge. On a paper cutter, a metal guide that works with the back gauge to square piles of paper before cutting. The side gauge is stationary and should be at a perfect right angle to the back gauge.

Side-sewing. A method of binding in which the entire book is sewn as a single unit, instead of as individual sections. Side-sewn books will not lie flat when open.

Side-stitch. A method of binding in which the folded signatures or cut sheets are stitched along and through the side close to the gutter margin. The pages cannot be opened fully to lie flat. Alternative term: *sidewire*.

Signature. A single press sheet that has several pages printed on both sides of it so that when it is folded the pages will appear in their correct order in a book or magazine. Signatures may consist of four pages, eight pages, sixteen pages, or some other multiple of four. Printed signatures have fold marks, indicated by broken lines, that are used to set up the folder.

Signature feeding station. See *feeder station*.

Skid. A type of pallet without bottom deck boards. See also: *pallet*.

Slitting. Cutting a sheet in a straight line along the traveling direction of the paper. Doing this on a folder can reduce the processing time on the job, because the product does not have to move to the cutting machine.

Smash. Heavy pressure used to compress a book so that it will have less bulk. See also: *nip; nipping*.

Smoothness. The measure of the evenness or lack of contour of a paper's surface. Smooth papers are considered to have better printability than less-smooth papers. Smoothness can affect bindery operations, especially when the paper is not smooth but textured. Smoothness can also affect paper stacking and feeding. Low-smoothness paper has less tendency to slip and slide, but too much texture and the paper may jam or slow some bindery operations.

Smyth sewing. Bookbinding by sewing thread through the backfold of a signature and from signature to signature. This links the signatures together, while permitting the opened book to lay flat.

Spine. The point of a multipage document where the pages are bound together.

Spiral binding. A mechanical binding method in which a continuous wire coil is run through a series of closely spaced holes near the gutter margin of loose sheets.

Split back gauge. On a paper cutter, a back gauge divided into three sections that allows a book to be trimmed on top, bottom, and one side without changing the cutter settings.

Stamping. See *hot foil stamping*.

Static. Electrical charges that cause sheets to cling to each other or to finishing equipment components, thus interfering with smooth feeding of sheets through equipment. Static problems are more pronounced with large lightweight papers and high-gloss papers.

Stitcher. See *saddle stitcher*.

Stitching head. The device on a saddle stitcher that drives the stitch through the upturned spine of the signature set on the saddle.

Stitching section. The portion of a saddle stitcher that includes a wire spool and a stitching head that drives the wire into the signature set.

Stock. Another name for paper used in the printing industry.

Tape guide bands. On a folder delivery, continuous narrow belts positioned beneath the catch rollers that together inch the folded sheets forward on the delivery table.

Template. A computer-generated page layout/design file that ensures each page in a document has a consistent look to it. This file sets up consistent margins, headers/footers, graphic elements, and typeface and type sizes to be used in the document.

Three-knife trimmer. Located after the stitching head on a saddle stitcher and after the nipping station on an adhesive binder, this device cuts each booklet on three sides to the product's final size.

Tip-on/tip-in machine. An auxiliary device for saddle stitchers or adhesive binders that secures or "tips in" inserts to signatures with a thin strip of releasable adhesive. Examples of products that are tipped in include reply cards, coupons, envelopes, and sample merchandise secured to the front and back pages of signatures. Alternative term: *tipper.*

Trim. The excess area of a printed form or page in which instructions, register marks, and quality control devices are printed. The trim is cut off before binding.

Trim marks. Guide marks on the printed sheet to indicate where the product will be trimmed on the cutter. Trim marks are usually indicated with a solid line that starts roughly 1/8 in. from final page size.

Trim size. The final dimensions of a page.

Trimming. Cutting a small amount of excess paper off the edges of a multipage product to neaten the ragged edges of printed pieces, open the closed edges of folded signatures, and bring printed material to its designed size. For flat sheet work (unfolded product), trimming to the finished sheet size follows presswork. Trimming can be done using a dedicated three-knife or five-knife trimmer, or a single-knife guillotine cutter.

Waste. Materials used in the print production process that must be discarded or recycled. Examples include proof stock, plates, and setup stock.

Web. A roll of any substrate that passes continuously through a printing press or converting or finishing equipment.

Web offset. A lithographic printing process in which a press prints on a continuous roll of paper instead of individual sheets.

Wet scoring. A special water attachment on a folder that applies a thin, straight stream of water where the paper must fold, as an aid in creating a clean fold.

Wire gauge. The thickness of the wire expressed in a special numbering system where smaller numbers indicate a larger wire diameter. Generally, wire used in saddle binding machines ranges from gauges 19 to 25.

Wire stitcher. See *saddle stitcher.*

About the Author

Like most people of a certain age, Frances Mavretic Wieloch has seen and interacted with print production in many forms for a lifetime that goes from orange-tinted faces on magazine covers to PDFs on the Internet. She has been a bona fide member of the printing industry, albeit on the editorial periphery, for more than nine years. She is also a long-time print customer and an experienced editor and writer about business and technical topics that range from computers and banking to metallurgy and materials science. She was the editor of *GATFWorld* magazine for eight years, editor of the annual *GATF Technology Forecast,* and editor of the Printing Industries of America's *Management Portfolio* newsletter. As the rest of you, she continues to learn about the changing print/graphic arts industry from people, print, and pixels. This is her first published book.

About GATF

The Graphic Arts Technical Foundation is a nonprofit, scientific, technical, and educational organization dedicated to the advancement of the graphic communications industries worldwide. Its mission is to serve the field as the leading resource for technical information and services through research and education. GATF partners with the Printing Industries of America (PIA), the world's largest printing industry trade association.

For 79 years the Foundation has developed leading edge technologies and practices for printing. GATF's staff of researchers, educators, and technical specialists partners with nearly 14,000 corporate members in more than 80 countries to help them maintain their competitive edge by increasing productivity, print quality, process control, and environmental compliance and by implementing new techniques and technologies. Through conferences, Internet symposia, workshops, consulting, technical support, laboratory services, and publications, GATF strives to advance a global graphic communications community.

The GATF*Press* publishes books on nearly every aspect of the field; learning modules (step-by-step instruction booklets); audiovisuals (CD-ROMs and videocassettes); and research and technology reports. It also publishes *GATFWorld*, a bimonthly magazine of technical articles, industry news, and reviews of specific products.

For more information on GATF products and services, please visit our website at www.gain.net, or write to us at 200 Deer Run Road, Sewickley, PA 15143-2600 (phone: 412/741-6860).

About PIA

In continuous operation since 1887 and headquartered in Alexandria, Virginia, Printing Industries of America, Inc. (PIA), is the world's largest graphic arts trade association representing an industry with more than 1 million employees and $156 billion in sales annually. PIA promotes the interests of more than 14,000 member companies. Companies become members in PIA by joining one of 28 regional affiliate organizations throughout the United States or by joining the Canadian Printing Industries Association. International companies outside North America may join PIA directly.

Printing Industries of America, Inc. is in the business of promoting programs, services, and an environment that helps its members operate profitably. Many of PIA's members are commercial printers, allied graphic arts firms such as electronic imaging companies, equipment manufacturers, and suppliers.

PIA has developed several special industry groups, sections, and councils to meet the unique needs of specific market segments. Each group provides members with current information on their specific market and helps members stay ahead of the competition. PIA's special industry groups are the Web Offset Association (WOA), Web Printing Association (WPA), Graphic Arts Marketing Information Service (GAMIS), Label Printing Industries of America (LPIA), and Binding Industries of America International (BIA).

The special sections and councils include Printing Industry Financial Executives (PIFE), Sales & Marketing Executives (S&ME), EPS—the Digital Workflow Group (EPS), Digital Printing Council (DPC), and the E-Business Council (EBC).

For more information on PIA products and services, please visit www.gain.net or write to 100 Daingerfield Road, Alexandria, VA 22314 (phone: 703/519-8100).

Additional Resources

Publications of Interest from GATF

For explanations of other print processes, the sequence of a nondigital workflow, or the printing process in general, see the following:

The Basics of Print Production. Mary Hardesty.

Computer-to-Plate Primer. Richard M. Adams and Frank J. Romano.

The GATF Encyclopedia of Graphic Communications.
   Frank J. Romano and Richard Romano.

Lithography Primer, Second Edition. Daniel G. Wilson.

On-Demand and Digital Printing Primer. Howard M. Fenton.

Pocket Pal: A Graphic Arts Production Handbook.
   Michael H. Bruno, ed.; International Paper.

To learn more about the many different kinds of imposition, see:

Understanding Digital Imposition. Hal Hinderliter.

For more information about the design and prepress areas:

Computer Color Graphics. Harry Waldman.

Document Design Primer. Pamela Mortimer.

The GATF Guide to Desktop Publishing, Third Edition. Hal Hinderliter.

Scanning Primer. Richard M. Adams.

To learn more about binding and finishing work and various related processes, see:

Binding, Finishing, and Mailing: The Final Word. T.J. Tedesco.

Direct Mail Pal: A Direct Mail Production Handbook. T.J. Tedesco,
   Ken Boone, Terry Woods, and John Leonard.

FOLD: The Professional's Guide to Folding. Trish Witkowski;
   Finishing Experts Group, Inc.

Materials Handling for the Printer. A John Geis.

A Short History of Binding. William Oresick.

Skill Standards: Finishing and Distribution.
National Council for Skill Standards in Graphic Communications

For a thorough explanation about paper in the pressroom, see:
Paper Buying Primer. Lawrence A. Wilson
What the Printer Should Know About Paper. Lawrence A. Wilson.

To learn about management and workplace issues, read:
Customer Service in the Printing Industry. Richard E. Colbary.
Frontline Supervision Primer. Don Merit.
Print Production Management Primer. Don Merit.
Print Production Scheduling Primer. Don Merit.

GATF Training Curriculums

The GATF Bindery Training Curriculum. Daniel G. Wilson.
PrintScape: A Crash Course in Graphic Communications.
Daniel G. Wilson, Deanna M. Gentile, and GATF Staff.

GATF Training Workshops

Orientation to the Graphic Arts. (5 Days)
Estimating, Scheduling and Production Planning. (3 Days)
Troubleshooting Bindery, Finishing & Mailing Problems. (2 Days)

Associations

Binding Industries Association International, 70 East Lake St., #300, Chicago, IL 60601. Phone 312-372-7606. Internet: www.bindingindustries.org.

Foil Stamping and Embossing Association, 2150 SW Westport Dr., Ste. 101, Topeka, KS 66614; telephone: 785-271-5816; Web: www.fsea.com.

Graphic Arts Technical Foundation/Printing Industries of America (GATF/PIA). GATF, 200 Deer Run Rd., Sewickley, PA 15143; phone: 412/741-6860. PIA, 100 Daingerfield Rd., Alexandria, VA 22314; 703/519-8100. Internet: www.gain.net.

Research & Engineering Council of NAPL, PO Box 1086, White Stone, VA 22578-1086. Phone: 804-436-9922. Internet: www.recouncil.org.

Colophon

At the Finishing Line: A Primer for New Bindery Workers was edited, designed, and printed at the Graphic Arts Technical Foundation, headquartered in Sewickley, Pennsylvania. The manuscript was written using Microsoft Word and QuarkXPress, and the files were sent to GATF. The edited files were imported into QuarkXPress 4.1 on an Apple Power Macintosh G4 for page layout. The primary fonts used for the interior of the book were New Caledonia, with heads in Myriad Tilt. Page proofs for author approval were produced on a Xerox Regal color copier with Splash RIP.

Upon completion of the editorial/page layout process, the illustrations were transmitted to GATF's Robert Howard Center for Imaging Excellence, where all images were adjusted for the printing parameters of GATF's in-house printing department and proofed.

The preflighted pages were printed to Agfa's Apogee production system. Agfa's Sherpa 43 was used to produce the digital imposed proofs for customer approval. Creo Preps was used to impose the pages, and then the book was output to a Creo Trendsetter 3244 platesetter. The interior pages were printed on GATF's 26×40-in., four-color Heidelberg Speedmaster 102-4P sheetfed perfecting press, and the cover was printed two-up on GATF's 20×28-in., six-color Komori Lithrone 28 sheetfed press with tower coater.

The cover sheets were folded on the Stahl folder before the interior pages and covers were sent to a trade bindery for perfect binding and final trimming.